Using Television in the Primary School

Using Television in
the Primary School

Ernest Choat and Harry Griffin

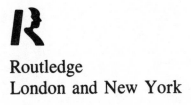

Routledge
London and New York

First published 1989
by Routledge
11 New Fetter Lane, London EC4P 4EE

© 1989 E.Choat and H. Griffin

Printed and bound in Great Britain by
Mackays of Chatham PLC, Chatham, Kent

British Library Cataloguing in Publication Data

Choat, Ernest
  Using Television in the primary school.
  1. Education. Role. Television
  I. Title II. Griffin, Harry
  371.3'358

  ISBN 0-415-04206-2

CONTENTS

FIGURES AND TABLES

FIGURES

TABLES

ACKNOWLEDGEMENTS

We are extremely grateful to all those teachers, head teachers and inspectors/advisers who have co-operated with us in our previous research and with our current work. Without their goodwill to look more closely at how they were using television, and to be far sighted enough to want to investigate how the medium could be used more effectively, then such a book as this would not be possible. In particular we are indebted to those head teachers and teachers who have consented to allow the practice in their school or classroom to be made known in the book.

We would also like to thank our colleagues Dorothy Hobart and Pascal Kivotos, Head of the AVE (Audio-Visual Education) Centre, University of London, Goldsmiths' College for their contribution and wisdom with our work, DS Information Systems and the Baring Foundation for their support to allow us to pursue our investigations in greater depth and last, but not least, our secretary Margaret Wise, who had the unenviable task of deciphering our writing to produce a legible script.

Ernest Choat
Harry Griffin

Chapter One

INTRODUCTION

The teacher glanced at her watch.

'Now, children. Stop what you are doing and line up at the door. It's time to go to television', she said.

Her announcement had a mixed reception. Some children stopped instantly and rushed to the door. Others were reluctant to stop their activity and resented the interruption.

'Come along, children,' the teacher repeated, 'Hurry up, otherwise we'll miss the start of the programme.'

The stragglers made their way to the end of the line. The classroom door was opened and the children made their way to the television set in the hall.

'Don't fuss, John,' the teacher remarked to a boy who was disputing his place in front of the screen with another boy. 'Sit down or you can go back to the classroom.'

John did as he was told. The other children carried out their regular routine and sat cross-legged in two straight rows across the hall. Meanwhile, the teacher was tracing the lead from the television set and, having located the plug, placed it in the wall socket and clicked the switch. As she made her way back to the television set another classroom door opened and children began to emerge. This class was not as orderly as the first and rushed to take their places.

'Sorry we're late, Miss Jones', said the second teacher. 'We almost missed it. We would have if Sally hadn't reminded me.'

Miss Jones had located the appropriate channel and switched on the television set. A clock face with a second hand making progress around the dial had attracted the attention of a few of her children, but others were content to play with their shoelaces or chat to their neighbour.

'Listen children, the programme is about to start. Pay attention', demanded Miss Jones.

The second class had now settled into their positions. All of the children, except John, looked up and stared towards the

1

screen.

'What are you doing, John?' Miss Jones asked, angrily. 'I've told you once. If you can't behave you can go back to the classroom. Look at the television.'

John did as he was told, and the programme began. The two teachers, each with a chair in hand, looked around anxiously and then decided to sit down together at the side of the hall. The children had been watching attentively for two minutes when the door at the back of the hall burst open. A swarm of children, attired in protective clothing from the rain, rushed in. Necks craned around to see what was happening.

'Sorry about this,' exclaimed the newly arrived teacher. 'Didn't know whether to come or not. It's raining so heavily and we have to come right across the playground. Thought it was a pity to miss it as we did some good follow-up after last week's programme.'

Mrs Smith stood around with umbrella dripping on the hall floor as some children began to undo their wet clothing while others sat down where they were.

'Hurry up, children,' she said, 'Mrs Brown's and Miss Jones's classes can't hear for the noise we're making.'

Soon the children had settled behind the other two classes and the teacher went across to join her colleagues. A brief, muffled conversation began between the teachers.

Not all of the children were giving their attention to the television screen. John, in particular, was more concerned with something which the boy next to him had in his hand and was trying to procure it. Miss Jones broke off her part in the conversation to observe John but was diverted by an exclamation from another child.

'I've got one of those, Miss,' he shouted across to her.

'All right, Paul. Tell me later. Look at the television for now.'

She craned her neck to look further along the line.

'Stop talking, Amanda. You can't hear what's being said if you're talking. Listen to the programme.'

Amanda did as she was told, but Miss Jones remained intent on John's activity. He and the boy next to him were still fidgeting.

'John and Roger, I've told you before and I'm not telling you again. Back to class the pair of you. You don't deserve to come and watch television.'

The two boys stood up and, weaving their way through the other children, reached the edge of the massed gathering. They stood motionless, looking directly towards Miss Jones.

'Off you both go. You heard what I said,' she admonished

in a stern voice.

Heads turned around as the two boys departed but a few children did not object to the diversion. In fact, they were pleased to have an opportunity to give their attention to something other than the television screen. Others were still watching intently, but the recently arrived class were finding it somewhat difficult to settle.

The fidgeting gradually became more widespread. The teachers looked at each other until Mrs Brown began to thumb the pages of the teachers' booklet and paused when she came to the page which related to the current programme.

The uneasiness continued until, with relief, the programme credits began to appear. Murmuring broke out among the children. The teachers stood up and turned to teach other.

'Don't think I'll do any follow-up of that,' said Miss Jones.

'Neither will I,' Mrs Brown responded. 'Got too much else to do.'

'I don't know. There were one or two useful things to follow-up,' said Mrs Smith.

Miss Jones walked across to switch off the television set where she waited while Mrs Smith's class prepared themselves to go back out into the rain. Meanwhile, Mrs Brown's class had risen of their own accord and were proceeding towards their own classroom. Preparations completed, Mrs Smith's class gradually made their way to the hall exit and with excited cries began to disappear.

Watching attentively, Miss Jones's class waited for her hand to be raised. When it came the children stood up, turned and followed each other towards their classroom. The door was opened, the children filed in and went back to their previous activities. Miss Jones entered and closed the door.

'I don't think we'll do any follow-up today. Get on with what you were doing,' she announced to the class.

When Mrs Smith's class arrived back in their prefabricated hut they took off their rainwear and sat down on the carpeted area. Mrs Smith moved her chair from the desk and sat facing the children with the teachers' booklet resting on her knees.

'Well, children, wasn't that a lovely programme,' she began. 'Did you enjoy it?'

'Yes-s-s,' some children murmured while others preferred to stay silent.

'Doesn't the milkman have to get up early,' said Mrs Smith.

'My dad gets up early,' replied a boy.

'So does my Dad,' echoed a girl.

'Yes, but they're not milkmen, are they?' Mrs Smith

responded, then continued, 'Who's been to a dairy?'

Spurred by the question, hands shot up. 'Jackson's Dairy, Miss,' the children shouted together.

'Jackson's Dairy, where's that?'

'Butterworth Road, Miss.'

'Butterworth Road, Oh, I know where you mean. But that's not a proper dairy. They only sell milk there, they don't process it like we saw on the television.'

The children were silenced.

'Where does the milk come from?' asked Mrs Smith.

'From the milkman,' a girl shouted out.

'No, not the milkman. Where does it come from in the first place?'

'From the cows,' someone shouted out.

'There weren't any cows.'

'But the milk lorry went to the farm to collect the milk.'

'There was a horse,' remarked a girl.

'Where was the horse?' enquired Mrs Smith.

'By the gate when the lorry went past.'

'I didn't see a horse, but we're not interested in horses. They don't give us milk,' added Mrs Smith.

'I like horses,' the girl said.

Although the events portrayed in this description may only occur in a minority of primary schools, mass viewing of television is by no means uncommon, irrespective of whether an off-air broadcast or video playback is used. Very little preparation is carried out prior to viewing. The children are assembled en masse to view irrespective of their levels of development or stages of progress. They are expected to maintain concentration for the full twelve to fifteen minutes' duration of the programme, and are not allowed to pass comment or make observations during the transmission but are expected to remain attentive. If follow-up is carried out it is related directly to the programme, not to the children's normal activities, and there is little attempt to link programmes in an educational television series.

USE OF TELEVISION IN SCHOOLS

As we discovered in our three-year national survey (Choat *et al.* 1987), television is not being used very effectively by many primary-school teachers, even when these teachers have access to a video recorder. Although several factors may contribute to this, the fact remains that the use of television in primary schools is a neglected issue. Sparse attention has been given to the desirability of the medium in curriculum considerations by those responsible for framing the curriculum and those responsible for carrying out the curriculum. In other words, television rarely features when aspects of the curriculum are debated or when teaching is planned. Furthermore, minimal concern has been directed towards the feasibility of using television to assist with the teaching of language, mathematics, and topic work, the three main areas of use in the primary school. It has been assumed that television is a suitable medium, so series are planned and programmes made to cater for these curriculum areas. Finally, minimal research has been carried out on the use of television as a learning tool for primary-school children. The accepted fact seems to be that large groups of children can watch a programme, the teacher discusses it with them and then follows it up according to a set pattern.

Those who use television in this way have failed to evaluate the use of television in primary schools. They fail to take into account the role that television should play in the operational curriculum and do not consider its function in children's learning. Television is a fruitful medium which can be used to advantage for both teachers' and children's benefit. It is a resource available to teachers to initiate or supplement the activities or work they are providing and can act as a form of motivation to assist with children's learning. However, it is essential for teachers to consider (a) why they are using television for certain areas of the curriculum, (b) whether the series and programmes intended for use fit in with the curriculum policies of the school, (c) if the material to be watched is conducive to the level of development of those children who will view it, and (d) how the viewing session will be incorporated into the children's normal activities.

Not a great deal of weight is given to these considerations by most primary-school teachers and it is the intention of this book to draw attention to them with the hope that television will be used more effectively. Furthermore, there are other circumstances towards which the book may be of some assistance. Television in the classroom has been a neglected issue both from a theoretical and practical point of view. It is rarely considered by those responsible for framing the primary-school curriculum (an issue which appears to be due for ministerial intervention according to Mr Baker, Secretary of State for Education) and those who write and deliberate on primary-school practice. Neither has the use of television featured in the training of most teachers or their subsequent in-service education. If only in a modest way, this book may help to fill the void.

SCHOOL RESOURCES

Even though the other factors might be resolved, the question of adequate resources has to be overcome. The majority of schools make do with only one television receiver (often a large set to enable a number of children to view at the same time). Possession of video recorders is on the increase with approximately three-quarters of primary schools now having such a machine, but most of these have been purchased through fund-raising activities or donations from parent-teacher associations. Through enumerating how television can be more effectively used than at present in most schools, we hope to encourage an increase of appropriate resources in primary schools.

RESEARCH INTO EDUCATIONAL TELEVISION

The Independent Broadcasting Authority began educational television broadcasts in 1964 for infant schools, and the British Broadcasting Corporation followed three years later. At the same time programmes were provided for junior and secondary children. A large number and variety of programmes are now produced for all children and almost all schools are using educational television, the vast majority viewing this in colour. Recently there has been a big increase in schools using video recorders. Almost all secondary schools possess at least one video recorder and many have more, while about 75 per cent of primary schools possess this facility although very few have more than one machine.

In 1983 the National Association of Head Teachers (1983:19) referred to educational television as the most powerful medium of mass communication that man has invented, and pointed out its tremendous potential as an educational tool if used carefully and with professional thought.

It is perhaps surprising, considering the amount of time spent using educational television in schools, that limited research has been carried out in this area. The School Broadcasting Council, Independent Broadcasting Authority and individual television companies conduct surveys through their education officers and research personnel but their findings are not usually made public. The IBA also publish the results of one-year Fellowships which they offer to teachers but these are rarely read by people in the classroom. A substantial enquiry was carried out in 1972/73 by Hayter, a retired HMI, on behalf of the BBC and IBA. Hayter (1974) set up his study with a simple hypothesis - a school interested and willing to explore the planned levels could achieve distinctive education gains for its pupils. He collected material from 106 schools through case studies and reports from head teachers and teachers and focused on eleven schools (primary and secondary) to report on the success of the experiment. Hayter showed what could be done with schools that had attention and support but this seemed to have little effect on the thousands of schools that did not have the support and were without the special facilities.

EDUCATIONAL REPORTS AND BOOKS IN RELATION TO EDUCATIONAL TELEVISION

The need for research into educational television was pointed out by Himmelweit, Oppenheim, and Vince (1958:64-6). In 1977 the Annan report (pp. 322-7), made a plea for more money to be spent in this area and The Bullock Report (1975:322-7) complained of lack of money to carry out research which they believed was necessary.

Apart from these research recommendations there has been little guidance in the use of educational television in the various reports that have been published. The Bullock Report recommended that educational television should help in providing a source of stimulus for talking, reading, and writing, but gave no further guidance. The Plowden Report (1967) stated that television was part of ordinary life and that children should be taught to use it for learning as well as entertainment. The Primary School Survey (1978) made only passing remarks and The Cockcroft Report (1982) merely added that mathematics programmes can form the basis of a course or supplement other work. The First School Survey (1982) was critical of the way many teachers were using educational television, but the HMIs did not suggest ways to overcome these deficiencies. Likewise, books have been published which theorize on the education of young children but omit to consider educational television. Dearden (1976) deals with the practical problems of primary education but does not mention television. Pluckrose (1979) examines the contents of the primary school curriculum and the philosophy underlines it but educational television is excluded. Blenkin and Kelly (1981) discusses the characteristics of progressive education and curriculum in terms of process, but no mention is made of the role of educational television.

Local educational authorities also pay scant attention to educational television in the curriculum recommendations. The Inner London Education Authority (1981) report on the primary schools curriculum gave no guidance on the use of educational television, in an otherwise very full report, and the Essex County Council's document on the significance and need for planning when teaching topics and centres of interest only made a passing reference to educational television.

INCORPORATING EDUCATIONAL TELEVISION INTO THE CURRICULUM UP TO THE AGE OF SEVEN YEARS, PROJECT

It was because of the lack of research into educational television that the Leverhulme Trust gave the authors of this book, assisted by Dorothy Hobart, funding to carry out research. This took place between 1983 and 1985 after a year's pilot study. The aim of the research was to discover how teachers in infant schools were using educational television and to what extent it was being incorporated into the curriculum. It was hoped that on the information we obtained from this research we would be in a position to give some guidance into the effective use of educational television with young children.

Research Method

Two hundred and sixty-two teachers took part in the research. They came from seventeen local authorities in England and Wales and, apart from a small number of nursery teachers, were all teaching children in the 5-7 year range. During the first year the teachers filled in four questionnaires relating to areas of the curriculum and also in the first term filled in a weekly checklist analysing the television programmes they were viewing. Groups were visited on five different occasions when the questionnaires they had completed were discussed. This provided a form of in-service training and also gave us valuable insight into their use of and attitude to television. Care had to be taken to minimize the effects of the in-service training on the research results, and only questionnaires that were completed before the in-service session were included in the final results.

In the second year of the project, case-history studies, some of which are reported later in the book, were carried out. The results stated below are all taken from the first year's research work.

Results of the survey

This was a very comprehensive study and the results were reported in detail in *Teachers and Television* (1987).

However, the main findings can be summarized briefly. Most teachers appeared to enjoy television which they thought enriched and reinforced their teaching. It was able to supply material that they were not able to obtain in other ways, which widened children's outlooks. The visual and auditory stimulus that could be supplied by television through animation, sound effects, trick photography, graphics, etc. could not otherwise be used by teachers and this created interests and stimulated children's imagination. Many teachers particularly appreciated some of the excellent nature programmes which they claimed improved their teaching in this area. Although there was some criticism by teachers, a general approval was expressed of the way the programmes were presented. There was also approval of the inclusion of stories which the teachers regarded as a valuable part of the programme. Most teachers found the teaching notes valuable, although there were some complaints that these were not always received when required, while a few teachers thought that some schools could no longer afford to buy them. Although the question was not included in the survey, many teachers in discussion groups pointed out that the service was free and in the present economic climate that was very important.

However, the research results revealed that there were problems in three areas which caused great concern to the authors. These were:

1 size of viewing and teaching groups and the matching of work to the children's needs and interests;
2 incorporation of television teaching into the curriculum;
3 the use of the video recorder.

Size of Viewing Groups

Most infant teachers would accept that each child should be

treated as an individual. This does not specify that all teaching is on an individual basis, it merely implies that each child should be recognized as an individual with activities and information provided at his or her level of development and suited to his/her pace of learning. There would be occasions when children were taught on a one-to-one basis but there are many other occasions when children are taught in groups and there are times when it is beneficial for all the class to participate. The teachers in the research group agreed with this and usually taught in this way.

However, this did not apply when using television: of the 262 teachers who took part in the research, only 10 allowed children to view television in small groups, and these teachers usually had some extra help to enable them to do this. No cases were reported where group television viewing had taken place in a classroom where children were engaged in other activities. Furthermore, 88 of the classes were involved in mass viewing where two or more classes were present. If this is typical of infant schools in general more than half the children in infant schools in England and Wales view television alongside children from another class. Some teachers claimed this was necessary because of the shortage of facilities available in schools. However, when it is considered that programmes are usually shown twice a week and there is a wide selection available this should only happen on rare occasions. It was also found that there was no significant difference in mass viewing between schools that possessed a video recorder and those that did not.

Matching of Work to Children's Abilities

Most of the programmes made by the broadcasting companies fall into three categories - language programmes, mathematics programmes and general interest programmes, which could form the basis of topic work. While a few teachers would like specialized programmes in areas like science and music, and these have sometimes been provided, most teachers are satisfied with this arrangement. There were claims made by many teachers that even though they used class or mass viewing, this did not matter because individual differences were catered for in the follow-up work. They accepted this was very different when using mathematical programmes. This seemed to be the main reason why only 30 per cent of teachers used mathematical series compared with 91 per cent who used them for language and 84 per cent who used general interest series. Only 10 per cent of teachers chose to monitor a mathematical series. They did not see the same problems of matching work to children's abilities when using language series.

The way these programmes were usually used was to view and follow-up as soon as this was convenient. Teachers had not usually seen the programme previously and even though different work was given to different sections of the class it was difficult to see how this was related to children's needs as it was not usually related to ongoing classroom work. They tended to rely on the teachers' booklets for their ideas. There seemed to be more effective matching when general interest programmes were used. This could spark off other work which enabled teachers to teach in the way they normally taught and individual needs could be better catered for. The type of series lasting about six weeks which formed the basis of topic work was very popular. BBC's *Watch* series and ITV's *Seeing and Doing* were examples of these and did lead to topic work. In fact one of the main criticisms by teachers was that these were over-directed and it did seem to result in similar work in most of the schools who used them.

However, not all general interest programmes were used in this way. Many were treated as separate programmes and followed up in a similar way to the majority of language problems. There was often a lack of continuity between programmes even when this was suggested in the teachers' notes. Again, a number of language problems and even some of the mathematical programmes were linked to ongoing work. Whether the follow-up work was matching the children's interests and abilities tended to depend on whether teachers related it to ongoing work and taught in their normal way, rather than on the particular category of programme. This did however occur with greater frequency with the general interest programmes.

Incorporating Educational Television into the Curriculum

It was the view of the research team that educational television should be used as a resource that fitted in with the teachers' work and as such should be incorporated into the curriculum.

With the teachers who took part in the research this seemed to occur in the following situations:

1   When the programme coincided with work that the teacher was doing. (This occurred quite often during special

occasions such as Christmas and Hallowe'en.)
2   When a series of programmes was specifically devised to form the basis of a topic or project work.
3   When a particular programme sparked off work in the classroom which could be carried on for a number of days or even longer.

However, it was rare for teachers to consider the use of television in the planning of the curriculum or in the planning of a topic. Teachers were usually committed to the viewing of a certain series and many opportunities were missed to use television as a supplement to the work they were doing.

Use of the Video Recorder

Access to a video recorder is of great value to a teacher for the following reasons:

1   *Timetable convenience* An off-air broadcast can be recorded and played back at a time suitable to the teacher.
2   *Use of the controls* This allows the teacher to stop and start the programme when appropriate, and allows children to interact with the teacher and with each other during the showing of the programme.
3   *Programmes can be previewed beforehand* This helps teachers in their follow-up work, and they can decide whether the programme will be of any value to the children.
4   *Schools can build up resource material* This can be used when relevant or when they plan to use it when certain topics are being taught.

In practice the vast majority of schools simply used the video recorder for timetable convenience. Only a few teachers used the controls when the programme was being shown and even fewer teachers previewed programmes. Some schools recorded programmes they particularly liked so they could view them when they would no longer be broadcast, but it was rare to find a school that had sufficient resources that could be used for any form of curriculum planning. There was also very little difference in usage between schools which had just obtained their recorder and those which had possessed one for a number of years.

The statement by the Cabinet Office Technology Advisory Panel (1986:13) that video recorders, once seen as having enormous potential for education, have settled into a low-key role and have had only a peripheral effect, seems to confirm our findings.

Problems for Teachers

Although we were very disappointed with our research findings we realize that teachers have great difficulties in changing their attitudes towards the use of the television, which is necessary if it is to be used to full effect. There is little encouragement given by educationalists and little attention given to the effective use of educational television either in initial or in-service training. Many schools are very poorly equipped and sometimes have to view television in very difficult conditions.

CONCLUSION

The impression must not be conveyed that every teacher of children up to the age of seven years was using educational television ineffectively. The research findings are not encouraging but a few teachers were showing what could be done with educational television, and how it could be used creatively and incorporated into the curriculum. There were also a few teachers who were making effective use of the video recorder, and schools which had good resource libraries that could be used for curriculum planning. In the second year of our research we were able to visit schools where good practice was taking place. During this year we also observed a number of junior teachers. From observations and discussions with inspectors, head teachers, and teachers concerned with junior education, it appeared that educational television in junior schools was used in a similar way to infant schools and that what could be said of teachers in infant schools could be applied to junior teachers, although we have not the research evidence to confirm this.

The authors are of the opinion that teachers could use educational television far more effectively than they do at present. Television teaching can be incorporated into the curriculum and it is possible to use small-group teaching without too much difficulty. In the following chapters we hope to demonstrate this, giving examples from teachers' work in the classroom. However, it is doubtful if much improvement will occur unless there is a change in attitudes to educational television by colleges of education lecturers and inspectors, advisers and teachers' centre wardens in local authorities, which should lead to an increase in pre-service and in-service education.

REFERENCES

Blenkin, G.M. and Kelly, V.A. (1981) *The Primary Curriculum*, London: Harper & Row.

Cabinet Office Information Technology Advisory Panel (1986) *Learning to Live with IT*, London: HMSO.

Central Advisory Council for Education (England) (1967) *Children and Their Primary Schools (The Plowden Report)*, London: HMSO.

Choat, E., Griffin, H. and Hobart, D. (1984) 'Investigating educational television and the curriculum for young children: some pilot phase features', *British Journal for Educational Technology*.

Choat, E., Griffin, H, and Hobart, D. (1987) *Teachers and Television*, Beckenham: Croom Helm.

Dearden, R.F. (1976) *Problems in Primary Education*, London: Routledge & Kegan Paul.

Department of Education and Science (1978) *Primary Education in England: A Survey by HM Inspectors of Schools (The Primary School Survey)*, London: HMSO.

Department of Education and Science (1982) *Education 5 to 9: An Illustrative Survey of 80 First Schools in England*, London: HMSO.

Department of Education and Science (1975) *A Language for Life (The Bullock Report)*, London: HMSO.

Essex County Council (1983) *Topics and Centres of Interest in the Primary School*, Chelmsford: Essex CC

Hayter, C.G. (1974) *Using Broadcasts in Schools*, London: BBC/ITV.

Himmelweit, H.T., Oppenheim, A.M., and Vince, P. (1958) *Television and the Child*, London: Oxford University Press.

Inner London Education Authority (1981) *ILEA Statement on the Curriculum for Pupils Aged 5 to 16*, London: ILEA.

National Association of Head Teachers (1983), *Language and the Primary School*, Haywards Heath: NAHT.

Pluckrose, H. (1979) *Children and their Primary Schools*, Harmondsworth: Penguin.

Chapter Two

USES OF EDUCATIONAL TELEVISION

HOW TELEVISION SHOULD BE USED

Although how television is used in primary schools is a cause for concern, it is equally important to consider when television should be used. It was pointed out earlier that many teachers have become conditioned to using television on a regular basis by taking a series each week, irrespective of whether the programmes are regarded as part of the curriculum or if they are meeting children's needs. On the other hand, some teachers reject the use of television. They allege that children are exposed to too much television at home, and school should not encourage them to watch further. This is a short-sighted view. Children need to be encouraged to look and listen carefully to television and to talk about what they have seen. This can come about only if they are guided wisely into treating television in this way and if it is not happening at home then school should make some effort to help them.

MEDIA STUDIES

There is now a strong movement to encourage media studies as part of the curriculum in primary schools but this is a subject in its own right where the media and its influence is examined and does not fall within the province of this book which is concerned with television's use within teaching. Nevertheless, by using television more objectively and involving children in a broadcast or video playback and by encouraging interaction and interpretation, then teachers are providing examples of how to diagnose television content.

TELEVISION AND CHILDREN'S EXPERIENCE

Some teachers may object to television on the grounds that they have insufficient time to cover other things let alone to include television programmes as well. This too may be dismissing television out of hand with little consideration for the role it might play. Wise use of television can make many things more meaningful to primary-school children. The vast majority of teachers rely on language as their teaching medium. They tell children things, ask them questions, expect answers and require explanations but this is often going on in a vacuum. Words are meaningless unless they are allied to experience and this is frequently lacking in children.

This does not mean that television will provide the experience or the necessary understanding but its use can supplement and help provide meaning. Television brings a visual representation, accompanied by sound and movement, into the classroom, and can continue for any length of time. For instance, it can show the effects of a windy day with trees blowing to and fro, waste paper scurrying along streets, waves lashing the seashore, washing flapping on the line, etc. The children have obviously experienced similar situations but it may not necessarily be a windy day when the topic arises during the course of their activities. With a video tape available, the teacher can resort to it to provide the feel of the situation rather than having to rely on mere descriptions. He or she could, by using the controls on the video recorder, pause and freeze-frame to show the height of the waves as they hit the seashore, run a short sequence so the children can see the movement of the washing on the line, etc.

Although this means the teacher must have access to a video recorder and be able to use it effectively it is hoped that before long nearly all primary schools will have a video recorder available and, as will be shown later, it is well within the capacity of the teacher to use it in this way either with a class or small group.

THE IMPORTANCE OF FIRST-HAND EXPERIENCE

Although it could be claimed that television cannot replace first-hand experience, it can add to that experience by making it more meaningful. It would be foolhardy to have children watching the movement of a stream on television and be given work to complete if a stream flowed by the school. The children should be taken to the stream to observe the flow.

There might be occasions afterwards when the use of a tape will clarify the experience or initiate work, but the actual experience has more meaning than when it is seen second-hand on television. Furthermore, experiments are possible with the actual experience that cannot be carried out with television. However natural the television pictures might be, use can be made only of that which has been filmed.

Of course, the alternative situation may sometimes arise. A teacher might wish the children to see something depicted on television before they actually experience it. For example, a visit could have been arranged to a farm. Showing a video or suitable programme beforehand could give the children some indication of what they were to see or allow the teacher to emphasize certain aspects which she wishes the children to note.

HISTORY AND CHILDREN'S EXPERIENCES

With the circumstances described, television is allied to experience but there are occasions when such is not possible. For instance, it is very difficult to relate history to school experiences because history is a record of past events and human affairs. Only a depiction of historical facts can be portrayed and this leaves much to the imagination but, without interpretation, this imagination is susceptible to false impressions. Obviously, interpretation depends upon the extent of interaction by the teacher and level of mental development of the children involved. A programme about the Romans can show how the Romans lived, but the extent and the way in which the programme is understood will vary enormously. For many infant-school children imagination will likely turn into fantasy without any connection with reality while some upper juniors will try to relate the situation with their own town or village. A visit to a Roman villa will add some evidence to the situation but even this relies on children's imagination. The footings of buildings and mosaics give some indication of what life was like in Roman times but these have to be added to substantially before a realistic picture emerges.

GEOGRAPHICAL, SCIENTIFIC AND NATURE ASPECTS

Similarly, geographical and scientific aspects can be brought into the classroom by television and, although these may be more aligned to reality than history, they could still rely on authenticity for understanding. Showing programmes on navigation seems to have limitations for infant-school children. Even with the added interpretations, the television depictions are difficult for the children to translate. Trying to get infant-school children to appreciate the technicalities of navigation and charting, with the accompanying scientific implications and the situation confronting Dr Livingstone in Africa, seems beyond the majority of them. The aspects will be treated either as explorations into fantasy or incomprehensible to the majority of infant-school children. This is contrasted with a unit of programmes on a fictional character such as Robinson Crusoe. Here imagination and fantasy are allowed to develop with many situations such as messages from bottles and the likely consequences; being deserted and fending for oneself; suddenly being confronted by another person who was unable to speak in one's own language, etc., all being played out. Thus, no specific geographical or scientific aspects are intended. The programmes are being used merely to stimulate children's imagination and are not trying to bring factual information into the classroom.

On the other hand, television is able to bring close-ups to view that are not seen as clearly with the naked eye, and these are particularly valuable in the geographical and scientific spheres.

Television is a valuable resource at a teacher's disposal that can add stimulation to children's activities. However, care must be taken that the material is relevant and able to be interpreted to the children who will view it. Preferably, it should concern aspects with which the children are familiar or with which practical experience can be aligned. Nevertheless, it must be borne in mind that television pictures can be deceptive, especially with regard to size, height, length and distance. For example, not many people have been fortunate enough to have seen a Golden Eagle. Television pictures may show the bird and even compare it in size to other birds but it is still difficult to gauge how large a Golden Eagle actually is. Problems with height can arise with things such as trees, buildings, etc. Length is hard to estimate unless one object is compared with another. Distance can be even more difficult, for a long-range shot may show far-off hills or even a horse in a field, but how far away these objects might be cannot be accurately assessed.

THE TOPIC APPROACH AND ITS INTEGRATION INTO THE CURRICULUM

Teachers should take account of the limitations of television within their interpretations but the assets outweigh the deficiencies and television can be most useful to assist with history, geography and science teaching. However, primary school teachers rarely teach along subject lines and most favour a centre of interest or project approach that enables the integration of curriculum content by following a specific topic. The centre of interest is pursued mostly in infant schools through a title such as the postman, trees, birds, pets, etc. The title is connected mainly by songs, stories, paintings, models and discussion. Play, creative activity, reading, writing and mathematics are not necessarily displaced but included when relevant. The criterion for a centre of interest therefore is to stimulate interest in the classroom for a week or even longer provided that interest is maintained by the children.

The centre of interest or topic approach is also used in most junior schools. It can emanate through either the teacher or the children as a result of a visit or something happening or an interest but more often than not the teacher chooses a topic to investigate. The outcome should not be predetermined as the children should follow their own interests, thus allowing various areas to branch out and develop from the main theme. This implies that a teacher should make preliminary plans of where development might lead and secure books and materials which will be available for the children to use but she should be prepared to elaborate on the leads and to amend the original plans. However, many teachers have definite intentions when planning a topic and usually keep to the original plans.

Subject specialization therefore is not the object of a centre of interest or topic and is replaced by the integration of curriculum content. Definition by subjects is thus not easy when a project is under way but children require proficiency in some subject areas if they are to benefit from their enquiries. They need to be able to read if they are to acquire facts from books, write proficiently if they are to give accounts of their findings and use mathematics to express and communicate ideas. In addition, a degree of ability in drawing, painting and modelling allows them to express their findings in a creative way. Moreover, there is the danger with a topic that some children may concentrate on narrow areas of enquiry and this does little for them if these areas are outside the subject in which they are deficient, while only certain subjects may be encountered and others under-emphasized.

TOPIC WORK AND ITS RELATIONSHIP TO CHILDREN'S ABILITY

Management of a topic and the integration of curriculum content are skilful operations for a teacher if she is to ensure that each child in a mixed ability class is achieving according to his/her ability. Management and organization need to be to the fore otherwise integrated work could degenerate into aimless pursuits. Ideas might be followed that are irrelevant to learning, activities undertaken for no apparent reason and discoveries explained for no useful purpose, but these should not be taken as reasons to reject the interdisciplinary approach. It has many advantages. The teacher is in a position to encourage academic and social integration between children and foster greater association between the children and him/herself to develop communication and to enhance learning. She/he has the opportunity to present challenge to the more able children while making provisions for the less able. This means specifying different objectives in the sense that each child is determining his/her own objectives by his/her level of ability and approach to learning and that the objectives fluctuate according to his/her development. This implies that the teacher should cater for the needs and interests of individual children during integrated work by having fluid expectations and providing challenge. In other words, the children should be able to practise concepts and skills previously acquired but have opportunities to enhance their learning.

We concluded from our research (Choat *et al.* 1987), that 84 per cent of the infant school teachers who participated made use of general interests series on educational television to pursue the teaching of a topic. If junior school teachers were questioned the percentage would most likely be similar. However, bearing the previous comments in mind, it is questionable whether the programme should be used to that extent for topic work. To reiterate, often the programmes were not incorporated into the curriculum but treated separately from it. There were occasions when the children were trying to follow two topics at the same time, one topic from television and the other instituted by the teacher. Frequently, the topic related directly to the material shown in the television programme through direct follow-up and only when a unit of programmes on a particular topic was shown was an attempt made to link programmes for continuity. Therefore, in many instances the topic taken from television was not incorporated in the curriculum but treated as a separate entity.

OBJECTIVES OF TOPIC WORK

Schools should have a policy for topic work but the extent to which it is planned as part of the curriculum and the degree to which television is considered is rather obscure. Although a topic should continue only for the length of time that the children are interested, limited investigation has been undertaken into how long particular topics presented on educational television should last. Teachers in the survey thought that about half a term was a suitable period for older infants but this was too long for the younger children. We would have probably got a different response from teachers of junior children.

The broadcasting of an educational television general interest or miscellany series therefore raises certain issues. First, it is necessary to establish the objectives of the series and the programmes within it. Should each programme have a particular objective or should a series contain a variety of programmes with different objectives so that teachers can select those suitable to their needs? If these are made explicit to teachers they are in a position to decide when to use a programme.

Second, are the programmes merely for general interest or should they form the basis of topic work? The problem arises as to whether a programme can be incorporated into the curriculum if it is intended for information only. Perhaps there are occasions when a programme that has no relevance to the curriculum could be taken but this should not become a regular practice, otherwise television is being used merely to fill in. On the other hand, if the programme is intended to form the basis of topic work then it should be presented in a way to enable this. Obviously, if a teacher has a video recorder she should preview programmes to ascertain whether they are suitable for her purposes and the way she intends to use them. She should consider whether a programme does provide sufficient scope to be fitted into what will be going on in the class, if the content is at the level of the children who will view to enable interpretation and whether relevant activities and experience can be provided with the follow-on. In this the teacher should not depend directly on the programme content but extend the activities to the children's present circumstances. For instance, reference should not constantly be made to what was happening to the greengrocer in a programme about him, but to the children's own experiences of visiting the greengrocer's shop.

It should be imperative for teachers to take these factors into account when they are contemplating using television to assist with topic work. But our research findings indicated that although the teachers seemed reasonably satisfied with the general interest series being broadcast, it was difficult to find examples of teachers who used them for planned topic work. Again, we must stress that much of this has been brought about by lack of guidance in initial training and inadequate resources. As a result there has been insufficient discussion and attention given as to when to use television. Teachers rarely question the material or protest to the broadcasters. They may express dissatisfaction among themselves or even abandon a series but rarely do they get down to making a formal complaint.

PLANNING OF TOPIC WORK

Nevertheless there were examples of how television could be used effectively if it happened to fit in with the work being done in school, and also examples of effective work where a topic had been suggested by the nature of the series, or how topics had been sparked off by a particular programme. There were no examples, however, of a topic's being planned in advance and programmes being used from any series that could be effectively fitted into the topic. The Independent Broadcasting Authority produced a chart for primary and middle schools with all the educational television programmes for the 1984/85 academic year listed under topic headings. This listed fifty-three topics and more than five hundred programmes that could be used in the various areas, but some are mentioned in more than one category. When it is considered that the BBC could also produce a similar list which would increase the programmes available, this indicates the vast amount of material available for topic work in the primary school even when the fact that some of the material listed is only suitable for older children in the middle school is taken into account.

This list was not available to the teachers who monitored television series in our research, so it is not known whether this would have had any effect on their planning. However, when teachers were questioned at a conference run in conjunction with the research, and the material was available, no teachers appeared to have made use of it and the majority was not aware the list had been produced. A similar reaction was received from twenty five teachers attending a course in the summer, 1987.

It does appear unlikely that teachers using off-air broadcasts, will plan topics with educational television in mind, unless they use direct suggestions from the teachers' notes accompanying the series. As more video recorders are obtained it is hoped that teachers will learn to use them more effectively and the use of television will become incorporated into the curriculum and into curriculum planning. A few teachers are able to do this at present and some examples of work of this kind, together with a discussion of the conditions required to enable this to become a much more common practice, will be discussed in following chapters.

We also discovered a large number of teachers using series for topic work that were intended for older children. The teachers alleged that no suitable series was being broadcast for the younger children so they reverted to what was available. A number of teachers also turned to language or mathematics series for topic work.

Thus, from our survey we concluded that educational television series could be thought to assist with topic work:

1 When a unit in a series is of sufficient duration to provide activities or work in a number of areas.
2 When a programme, or perhaps two programmes, indicates associated activity work may last for one or two weeks or even longer. Some infant school teachers believe that one week is sufficient especially with younger children in the infant school.
3 When a particular topic is being taken and an educational television programme provides material for use with the topic. Sometimes this occurs fortuitously and at other times, such as Hallowe'en and Christmas, programmes are broadcast specially for the festival.
4 When a topic is planned in advance and programmes from any series are used that can be effectively fitted into the topic.

Again it must be emphasized that following these guidelines would produce more effective work if a video recorder were available. The video provides flexibility, and teachers are not restricted to the times of off-air transmissions, the continuous broadcast and constraints on selection of the material. Moss (1987) refers to educational television as a free resource for schools offering a year-round weekly average of nearly seven hours of broadcasting. He further states that the importance of ITV and BBC educational television services is greater than ever in view of recent developments in educational policy, changes in the curriculum, and the demand that schools should prepare children more effectively for adult life. This may be so, but teachers must make judicious use of the material if Moss's views are justified.

LANGUAGE DEVELOPMENT

Language may facilitate the expression and communication of knowledge but language development is more complex than isolating single aspects which may accrue, even from television broadcasts. What their actions and experiences mean to children can be expressed only through language but this is not achieved unless they employ logic to rationalize their thoughts. This comes about by conceptualization of their experiences and attaching the relevant word to identify the concepts. Words therefore are symbols which, when joined together, denote situations to others that have been deduced by thought.

Consequently, language is a system of agreed sounds which symbolize objects, processes, relationships, etc. which convey meaning and in turn facilitate interaction between individuals through interpretation of the symbolized forms, i.e. sounds. Language development therefore is the increase in capability to structure language to achieve explicit meaning of what is being expressed and communicated. On the other hand, there are structures, i.e. language skills, which have to be learned to produce and receive the symbolized forms. These are phonology (sound systems such as phonemes or individual sounds), intonation (pitch), stress (emphasis), lexis (vocabulary) and grammar (rules which classify words by type to enable them to be put together, i.e. syntax (the order of words) and accidence (the changes made in individual words). Grammar therefore describes a language and classifies its words by type while specifying the rules for putting words together to make sentences.

Oracy, being the spoken language, is extended into literacy to allow reading and writing but further skills need to be acquired. The coded system is depicted in printed form so additional skills such as letter identification, word-shape identification, letter order, letter position, and sound identification of letter, group or word, need to be learned. The skills are then employed with reading methods which may be the sight, the whole word, the sentence, phonic or alphabetic method.

Although the skills provide for competence in language, children develop language within the content of meaningful use. Language develops as a result of an increasing awareness of the functions of language, i.e. using language to express feelings, to make contact, to identify, explain, describe, persuade, etc. Language therefore is learnt by hearing it being used effectively in a variety of situations and by actively participating in trial-and-error processes which allow complex linguistic rules to be worked out. The feedback enables children to know whether they have used language correctly. They are provided with linguistic information regarding new experiences and supplied with the relevant symbolization to attach the newly required conceptualization. Spurred by motivation and interest, children utilize this information and experiment with language until they gain command of it. The world presents such an array of new experiences for children that it begs to be put into words. Their natural curiosity constantly meets something new and they seek to identify it for themselves and for others.

The early learning of language occurs naturally and without formal instruction and results from the need to learn language in a variety of ways. Nevertheless, some children do find difficulty in learning the language skills taught in school. Teachers have a tendency to separate language from experience to make it more manageable whereas children do not separate language from the ordinary events of their lives; for them it is part of living. Language can become divorced from reality when it is separated so some children begin to reject the artificial language of school. They believe that they are being taught a subject rather than helped to use language for communication.

ROLE OF THE TEACHER IN LANGUAGE DEVELOPMENT

Teachers have a vital role in the development and refinement of children's communication ability. In addition to the curriculum related content, they should encourage children to communicate in an environment which provides the feedback necessary to develop language and improve the skills. A teacher has a responsibility to help children to understand how language works and what makes communication effective.

Whatever is done should be aimed at helping children to use the oral and written forms of language. Equally important is the need to encourage children to want to communicate effectively.

ROLE OF TELEVISION IN LANGUAGE TEACHING

It is within these considerations that teachers must assess if, and when, television can be used to assist with language teaching. Paramount within the considerations is whether television should be used for language development or language skills. We concluded in our research that most teachers insisted that they pursued a policy of language development but when the use of television was investigated it appeared that emphasis was directed towards language skills, especially reading skills.

Claims are made that television exercises and develops reading skills such as shape recognition, distinguishing between pairs of shapes, left to right sequencing, pictures and symbols, initial letter sounds, word combinations and difficult spelling combinations. These skills can be demonstrated by a presenter or depicted by animation or puppets to provide representation of them but the effect is questionable. Even though teachers may claim that they are not relying on television to teach the skills to children but using it as a supplement to their own work, it is difficult to envisage the effect continuous programmes might have on children watching en masse or as a class. The tendency is for children to ignore print when it is contained within a dramatized sequence. Their attention is captured by the action of the event rather than the representation. Alternatively, a direct approach of letters, words, and words forming sentences may be attempted on a blank screen but these depictions last for only a few seconds. Nevertheless, Fowles (1976) argues for the use of television for reading development and bases her claims on the following criteria:

1 Television has a positive attraction for children who generally associate the medium with pleasant experiences.
2 Television has great powers to capture, hold and direct attention.
3 Repetition, which is useful to slow learners, can be effectively utilized by television.
4 Children not only listen to songs in television programmes but they tend to memorize and sing them later.

5 Television can present the same simple instructional goal in many guises.
6 The first step towards literacy comes with the insight that print in some way conveys meaning. Television thereby can be used to convey a principle which is otherwise supremely difficult to explain to young children in a concrete visual mode that is consistent with the level of intellectual functioning.
7 Television is an audiovisual medium in which the visual image is dynamic.
8 Television not only draws attention to the screen generally, but careful design of the stimulus display permits control of visual scan patterns.
9 Television has a visual advantage when letters printed on the screen can be moved, lighted up, pulsated, coloured, or whatever to signal their correspondence with a phonemic segment. Highlighting of successive letters (or diagraphs) as a word is slowly pronounced reveals to a child how the word is to be perceptually broken. Seeing this happen many times, with many different words, will eventually reveal the code's structure. The specific strength of television is in directing a child's visual attention to the precise graphic unit corresponding to what he or she hears.

Tierney (1980) believes that greater attention to the potential of television could lead to a better integrated programme for the teaching of reading. She believes that vocabulary skills can be acquired through specially constructed programmes and that a carefully planned television curriculum for reading would reduce repetitive drills in the classroom. Tierney, along with others, bases much of her contention on the outcome of the American series, *Sesame Street* and *The Electric Company*, whose goals are to teach skills through imitation. To suggest that television becomes a creative teacher through *Sesame Street* programmes is rather an exaggeration. Split-second timing, images quickly following each other and drill sequences can hardly be regarded as creative. Furthermore, the use of stereotype worksheets when each child follows up with exactly the same work cannot be considered creative either.

LANGUAGE LEARNING FROM TELEVISION

Thus, it is difficult to conceive how a continuous programme emphasizing reading skills might benefit a whole class of

27

children at various stages in the acquisition of skills. Different children will have different needs while doubt remains as to the extent to which direct learning is possible from television. Even meaningful stop/start with the video recorder is not a practical proposition for a teacher who still has the whole class to contend with.

Small group viewing does have advantages, for the teacher is in a position to interact with what is shown and interpret it to the children but the question of whether television is a suitable medium for teaching skills still arises. In other words, television is no longer teaching. The teacher uses television as part of his/her teaching equipment when he or she operates the video controls with small group viewing and has to assess whether this has more effect on young children's learning than the orthodox methods which would normally be employed. The teacher has to take into account the techniques which television can offer compared to what she or he can provide, and weigh up the advantages and disadvantages.

READING DEVELOPMENT

Reading development is a different proposition to reading skills. Series designed for this purpose aim to encourage children to develop flexible reading strategies and an interest in books both for pleasure and information. Programmes can feature authors, books, and magazines as well as children themselves talking about their reading habits. Such programmes are more suited to upper junior schools children but yet again the teacher must not abdicate her role to television. She still has a function to play as interpreter and the children will naturally be influenced by how she reacts to the programmes. Standing back and allowing a programme to stand on its own will not promote as much stimulation as when a teacher interacts.

THE IMPORTANCE OF STORYTELLING

The aspects of reading development stem from children's earlier appreciation of story. Young children are always captivated by a well-told and interesting story, and reading or telling stories to the children is a common activity in infant schools and with lower junior school children, where it is often a daily occurrence, while poetry and literature feature more prominently with upper junior school children. Not only are fantasy and imagination exercised through stories and poems but children encounter new words and phrases and begin to appreciate the power and beauty of language.

While an included story of rhyme is often connected to the theme of an educational television programme, it is not really known how much this adds to the understanding of the theme. It is invariably enjoyed by the children and the inclusion is usually enjoyed by the teacher, most of whom regard it as an important part of the programme. In fact, a number of teachers would welcome programmes that were wholly devoted to story.

Storytelling should take a great deal of preparation and practice, often more than teachers are able to devote to it, while certain qualities of voice and a dramatic flair add to the impact and these are not possessed by every teacher. Television can bring skilled, professional storytellers into the classroom and help a teacher who is uncomfortable telling stories herself while expanding the range and opportunities for other teachers. There is no reason why children should not be encouraged to enjoy stories both from television and from their teacher. They then have the experience from an actual person and from an indirect source.

STORYTELLING AND TELEVISION

However, a Brown (1986:18-19) explains, children must keep up with the passing flow of words but have no control over their speed when listening to a story. She believes that listening to words alone limits their understanding and, with no additional cues from pictures, sound effects or music, they may be unable to decipher new words or complex sentences. To understand a story in any medium requires making all kinds of inferences from the grammatical to the logical. Thereby, Brown (pp.67-77) feels that stories on television have advantages over stories read or told by the teacher. She alleges that the change from the printed page to moving pictures affects the story content. Moving pictures depict some parts of a plot more readily than others, but once the pictures move children can see what characters are actually doing and have a base on which to assess their nature. The visual content also reveals to them the actions and the plot of the story in a way that can be grasped easily.

However, and Brown concurs, television stories do have some limitations. Accepting a screen image too literally can confuse children about objects and events. The sections of a plot selected by the producer can change the emphasis of the original story or give a different slant. For instance, the story of *Robinson Crusoe* was shown in an educational television series but Man Friday was left out. Joining two pieces of film or video tape transports a story's action from one place to another regardless of whether a character moves to another room or planet.

Within children's appreciation of stories from television there remain the factors previously enumerated that are associated with television viewing. Regardless of how well a story is depicted on television, interpretation by the teacher is still necessary. Television techniques might lead to distortions and these have to be explained. When asked to talk or write about a story, children must translate picture information into words. Some meaning is inevitably lost when one set of symbols is used to explain another whereas verbal story content needs only to be repeated. Nevertheless, apart from the aspects of story appreciation, a teacher has an opportunity to foster language development through his or her interaction.

STORYTELLING AND COMPREHENSION

Research evidence suggests, and a small survey carried out by Choat and Griffin (1986) seemed to confirm this, that children prefer stories viewed on television to stories read or told by the teacher, but the teacher's function is crucial if language development is to materialize. She needs to select the right material, undertake preliminary work and be conscious of eye control, gestures and reader-audience involvement when dealing with the story herself, but not all of these can be applied when using television. Selection of the right material and preparation are still essential but personal involvement is lacking. The teacher must therefore compensate for this, since comprehension, and hence language development, does not occur by just viewing stories on television. It does occur when stories are interpreted and discussed with children and when careful account is taken of their view in creative and original ways. We concluded that the most noticeable gains in language development were made in children's ability to comprehend the meaning of the story, and be orally creative when producing adaptations of stories, but this depended on effective small-group teaching.

A story occurring during the course of a programme does not lend itself to appropriate teaching as does a specially selected story. The programme story is normally associated with the content of the programme and is sometimes difficult to isolate whereas many teachers would prefer to have a stock of stories to use at their will. Also, we concluded that viewing television stories was more effective in aiding recall than hearing stories told or read by teachers, but this does not seem to rely on the teaching skills outlined previously.

A video recorder provides a teacher with a means of being able to replay parts of a story at the children's request or to emphasize certain features of the story. The teacher however must use discretion when doing this and not attempt to stop/start too frequently, especially in the initial playing of the story, otherwise she will interrupt the flow.

The video also enables those teachers who wish to use only the story in a programme to ignore the remainder of the programme material. In fact some teachers in our research indicated that this is what they did. This suggests, and several teachers supported it, that there is a case for the provision of story video cassettes to be used in all areas of the curriculum. These could be used in class, group, or individual situations by the children similar to the way in which books and audio cassettes are used at present. It must also be emphasized that story books should be provided for the stories viewed, as this links television with the printed word - and many children will want to read the story themselves.

Children of all ages always enjoy stories and this enjoyment is of paramount importance. There are some stories and rhymes told or read to them where the enjoyment may be greatly diminished if they are analysed too closely. Making these stories available on video cassettes can enhance the enjoyment by the use of television techniques but most stories can be used for the purpose of improving children's comprehension and language development. If teachers use television wisely for telling or reading stories, they should be able to improve children's comprehension without diminishing the enjoyment and this could be a valuable aid to the children's learning in many areas of the curriculum.

STORYTELLING AS AN ACQUISITION OF LANGUAGE SKILLS

It must not be overlooked that stories on educational television are also used for the acquisition of language skills. These can be either a single story that emphasizes a certain letter, letter combinations, sentence construction, etc., directly related to the story, or a serialized story which is geared towards sight vocabulary, phonic skills, language patterns and conventions, morphemic structure, and context areas. These programmes have a place but teachers must be careful in how they use them. The motivation accrued from the story or serialization can be destroyed with over-insistence on attaining the skills which the producer feels have been provided in a programme, especially if the follow-up procedure is to complete a worksheet.

As mentioned previously, television should be aligned to suit individual children's needs and this means that the skills associated with a particular programme should be aligned with only those children to whom the skills are relevant. Thus, the story element could be suitable to a small group or class of children but the related skills restricted to just a few of them. This is a case for individual interaction on video when an assignment is plotted for those children to whom it is relevant, but attention should also focus on language development. Of course, all of these necessitate planning and previewing of video tape material.

THE USE OF GENERAL INTEREST PROGRAMMES FOR LANGUAGE DEVELOPMENT

Language programmes, and the stories within them, can be most useful to assist with language teaching but it should be remembered that these programmes do not monopolize language. Many opportunities are presented through topic work on television to enhance language when this is integrated into normal activities and followed on.

MATHEMATICS AND THE NECESSITY FOR INDIVIDUAL EXPERIENCE

The use of television to help in teaching mathematics poses many problems for the teacher. Mathematical development is rooted in children's physical, mental, emotional, and social activities when they distinguish relationships and recognize correspondence to classify and order experiences. Thus, mathematics does not exist until it is created by an individual and results from accumulated experiences that enable him/her to rationalize and deduce to define the mathematics. Nevertheless, children in school rely on their teacher to provide activities from which experience, and hence mathematics, may be acquired. Consequently, as mathematics is individual to children, they should be regarded individually in their mathematical development. They will vary in their mathematical and intellectual ability, learn at different rates and be at various stages in their mathematical development. It is imperative, therefore that primary school teachers should be aware of how children acquire mathematics, factors which are likely to retard mathematical development, features related to progression in mathematics and the uses to which mathematics might be put.

There are certain psychological considerations to be taken into account, the most important being that children will not enhance their mathematical capability or become proficient in problem solving unless they are encouraged to acquire mathematics through understanding. This can be achieved only through concept acquisition and not by learning computation processes by rote. Concepts cannot be taught, they are acquired when patterns of relationship are formed through the mathematics inherent in children's experiences. This means that children must represent, deduce, rationalize, and realize in their minds if they are to understand relationally in mathematics and a teacher's task is to provide opportunities for activities and experiences to enable relational understanding to materialize. In other words, merely telling children does not ensure relational understanding in mathematics for, by telling a child, a teacher is trying to teach concepts.

MATHEMATICS AND TELEVISION

It is within this context that mathematics and television must be considered. Television is an abstract medium and mathematics, in its earlier stages, is defined by a series of abstractions taken from concrete experiences. Therefore, mathematical depictions on television require children to abstract from an abstraction. This may be possible in later stages of mathematics for, in fact, higher levels of mathematics require abstractions on abstractions, e.g. algebra, trigonometry, graphical representations, etc., but it is not feasible with young children who are only at the elementary stages in their acquisition of mathematics.

There was a certain amount of disquiet amongst the teachers whom we researched in their relationship with television and mathematics. Compared to the large extent that the medium was used for language and topic work, only 37 per cent used television for mathematics. A third of the teachers who objected did so on the grounds that mathematical development was individual and this could not be achieved through television. However, it must be pointed out that most of these teachers were referring to off-air broadcasts and the situation might be different if they had had access to a video recorder. Other teachers did refrain from using television because they were in sympathy with the psychological principles outlined previously and believed that mathematics should be acquired through experience.

MATHEMATICS SERIES AND THEIR RELATIONSHIP TO THE CURRICULUM

Nevertheless, when diagnoses were made of how television was being used we concluded that little attempt was being made to incorporate programmes into the curriculum, emphasis was directed towards number and number-related aspects, follow-up was normally a structured exercise and language was considered as the integral element in mathematics. In fairness to these teachers it must be said that proficiency in number appeared to be the objective of the educational television series that they were using but, on the other hand, this did appear to be the basis on which these teachers judged the value of a series.

When the opinions of all the teachers in the survey were gathered, the mathematics series were not highly thought of. They were generally considered to be a hotch-potch with too many mathematical notions included in each programme and were lacking in direction. The teachers would have liked just one notion, treated in various ways, to last for a few weeks with fewer studio sequences and greater concentration on activities in children's normal surroundings.

Television should show mathematics as exciting, practical, implicit in the environment, and a common language. Opportunities should be presented that enable ideas to be taken up by the teacher for interpreting to the children. Then these will be followed-on through practical activities to encourage understanding and conceptualization apart from catering for the application and extension of skills. Thereby television is not a means for the direct teaching of mathematics but a resource to support and extend activities begun by the teacher according to children's needs and levels of development.

These deliberations question the validity of mathematics series on educational television for primary school children. In their present form the series do not seem to fulfil any useful function. They are rather like a teacher trying to explain mathematics and are inclined to encourage rote learning. The series may aim to present a range of mathematical activities which can be incorporated into a mathematics scheme but are all of the children watching at the level of mathematical development depicted in a programme? As with all forms of development, children will be at various stages in their mathematical development and any one programme will be suitable for only a minority of them, emphasizing the need for small-group viewing and teaching according to levels of mathematical development.

MATHEMATICS AND THE USE OF TELEVISION

Further problems do arise even when small group viewing is practised. As the creation of mathematics takes place in the mind, children have to be allowed time to internalize. This is practically impossible with a continuous programme for no sooner are they attempting to work out one thing than the programme has gone on to something else. This is further complicated by the fact mentioned earlier that the children are trying to make their internalizations from an abstract medium. Therefore, two stages of mental analysis are being attempted, (a) to relate the television depiction to their own experiences, and (b) to interpret this translation into a situation that they understand and which has meaning to them. This may be possible for some junior school children but is hardly likely with infants.

For instance, a situation is presented whereby six apples have been bought at the greengrocer's. Mother takes them home and puts them on the kitchen table. Sandra appears, looks at the apples and asks how many she is going to have, Mother takes the apples and, while distributing them on the table, says, 'One for you, one for Daddy and one for Mummy. Another one for you, another one for Daddy and another one for Mummy. How many apples have you got?'

'Two.'
'How many has Daddy got?'
'Two.'
'How many has Mummy got?'
'Two.'
'How many have we each got?'
'Two.'

The producer is trying to depict a real-life situation with which many children will be familiar but children are being required to relate directly the decomposition of sets into a numerical operation. This is a long process for many children and is acquired only after an accumulation of experiences has provided them with the necessary logic to make the internal representation. It could be alleged that the television depiction is adding to the experience and is an alternative means of stimulation but the children could just as well be carrying out the activity themselves. They should have experience in a situation which means something to them.

The question therefore is whether defined mathematics on television does serve any useful purpose. Television does have the capacity to present movement and movement has an integral role to play in mathematics. It is also important to portray environmental situations in which the nature of mathematics is implicit. However, as many teachers pointed out, the assistance that television could give to teachers in the teaching of mathematics could be portrayed in the language and general interest programmes, providing producers had this in mind in the making of programmes. In fact some teachers did use them in this way and they questioned whether there was a need for separate mathematics programmes to be made.

CONCLUSION

The matters which have been discussed in this chapter have indicated that when television is used is just as important as how the medium is used. Television has been neglected in curriculum considerations both by those inside and outside primary schools. Too much faith has been placed in television to teach, whereas its rightful function is to be a resource to assist teaching. The following chapters give further suggestions to this end.

REFERENCES

Brown, L.K. (1986) *Taking Advantage of Media*, London: Routledge & Kegan Paul.

Choat, E. and Griffin, H. (1986) 'Young children, television and learning: Pt. 2 Comparisons of the effects of reading and story telling by the teacher and television story viewing', *Journal of Educational Television*, 12:91-104.

Choat, E., Griffin, H., and Hobart, D. (1987) *Teachers and*

Television, Beckenham: Croom Helm.

Fowles, B.R. (1976) 'Teaching children to read: an argument for television', *The Urban Review*, 9:114-20.

Moss, R. (1987) '30 years on', *The Times Educational Supplement*, 8 May, p. 36.

Tierney, J.D. (1980) 'The evolution of televised reading instruction', *Journal of Communication*, 30:181-5.

Chapter Three

OFF-AIR BROADCAST

MEANS OF VIEWING

In our survey over half the teachers were in schools that had
only one television receiver. A further quarter of the group
possessed two receivers, but one of these was an old black-
and-white set that was only used in an emergency. The
receiver was often placed in a central place such as the school
hall, and children had to leave their classroom in order to
view. A number of these sets were large and cumbersome to
move and were not very suitable for viewing purposes as the
screen was too high for the children who usually sat on the
floor. A smaller receiver placed on a trolley could have been
easily moved into the classroom when required and would
have been better for viewing. This would mean that all
classrooms would need to be equipped with power points and
aerial points but with the increasing use of audio-visual
equipment in school this would seem to be a necessity.

A number of schools had very poor facilities for viewing.
Some schools were on two levels and only had one large
television set which could not be moved between floors.
Another school visited had the television room at the far end
of the playground, and in inclement weather, children had to
put on outdoor clothing before they were to view a fifteen-
minute television programme. While it is appreciated that
primary-school budgets are very limited, schools with these
problems need to have a second television receiver.

CHOICE OF PROGRAMME

The normal practice in primary schools, which has changed
little over the years, is for teachers to choose, usually in
discussion with the headteacher, one, two, or occasionally

more series to be viewed on a weekly basis. Teachers were usually allowed to choose their favourite series providing it was suitable for their age group, but this rarely took into account other work they intended to do in the classroom. The main purposes for making these arrangements was that teachers' booklets could be ordered and classes could be allocated suitable times for viewing. Teachers tended to remain faithful to the series unless they were seeing a new series which did not come up to their expectations. They missed certain programmes if they felt there was other classroom work that was more important. This often occurred during the Christmas period when teachers were busy with other work. However, this was also the time when television tended to be integrated into other work in the classroom, as many of the programmes at this time showed material associated with Christmas. Only in about 1 per cent of the programmes mentioned did teachers claim they did not view the particular programme because the material was unsuitable for the children.

FORMS OF TEACHING

This organization tended to produce a stereotyped form of teaching. The class would view the programme sometimes with another class or classes present, and follow up either in the viewing area or in the classroom. This usually consisted of a short discussion of what was seen in the programme and follow-up work was given. Most teachers tried to give different work for children of different abilities, but this was very difficult as the teachers did not have much opportunity to prepare this until after they had seen the programme. Teachers' booklets were found to be very valuable for this purpose and most of the teachers were influenced by the suggestions given. These booklets were also found valuable by about three-quarters of the teachers for preparing children before viewing, although some booklets were rated very valuable for this purpose while others were considered of little value. Some teachers did not consider preparation was necessary before viewing, and this was stated by a large percentage of the small group who monitored mathematics programmes. None of the teachers viewed the programme before it was seen by the children, although some of the teachers may have seen the programme in a previous year. The preparation/broadcast/follow-up technique or the broad-cast/follow-up technique was used by the vast majority of teachers, and this did not differ significantly between teachers who had access to video recorders and those who did not. Only a small number of teachers used the video recorder for any other purpose than timetable convenience.

EFFECTIVE USE OF OFF-AIR BROADCASTS

Based on the results of the research and classroom observations, it is the opinion of the authors that to make full and effective use of educational television it is necessary to make full and effective use of the video recorder. Because this book is mainly concerned with development and change, emphasis in the following chapters will be on the use of video recorders. Nevertheless, there will be some teachers who will not have access to video recorders, as apart from the schools which do not have recorders, there are some large junior mixed and infant schools which only possess one machine and this may not be available to all the teachers who require it. Although research suggests that most teachers were using off-air broadcasts without relating this to other work in the classroom, there were exceptions. A number of teachers had viewed the occasional programme that had sparked off work in most areas of the curriculum. Groups of programmes of five or six weeks' duration caused many teachers to depart from their usual procedure and produce work in various areas for a few hours each week. These programmes, however, did produce work of a similar nature in a number of schools, and some teachers were concerned that television was dictating their teaching.

INCORPORATING TELEVISION INTO THE CURRICULUM

There was a very small group of teachers in the survey who were consciously integrating into the curriculum and using off-air broadcasts effectively. Two teachers had given some very good examples of this when they had monitored programmes and it was decided to study their work in depth. Visits were made to the classroom and the good results they achieved were seen. Details of the study will be given in the rest of the chapter to indicate what can be achieved even without the use of a video recorder.

GENERAL BACKGROUND

Both teachers were teaching in South Wales and attended the in-service sessions which were conducted in conjunction with the research. One teacher, Mrs A, taught in a small junior mixed and infants school on the outskirts of a small town. The school was semi open-plan and opened in 1983 on the merger of three very small schools. Mrs A was deputy-head teacher and taught a middle age-range infants class of twenty-seven children. (She used a language series during the autumn term 1984 and a general interest series when it began broadcasting in the spring term 1985.) Mrs B also taught twenty-three middle age-range infants in a five-teacher infants school situated in the midst of a council-housing estate in a large town. Many of the children's fathers were unemployed owing to the closure of the local steel works and eighteen children received free dinners. She used only one educational television language series.

CASE STUDY A: HOW SERIES WERE USED

Mrs A rarely used the teachers' booklet after a programme. The subsequent activities were primarily planned by her as follow-on according to the children's needs. Sometimes an event arose during a programme that interested the children and was taken up, but basically most activities were connected with other activities the children were doing. Figure 3.1 indicates how this was approached. Although this was a language series, Mrs A used it to incorporate many aspects of the curriculum. Her approach with the general interest series was similar. Although the programmes from the two series were in no way connected, Mrs A often found a way to link them to the children's activities. This was noticeable in all her work with television. For instance, discussion often related instances in one programme to another and a counting rhyme on sows and piglets which arose from the language series was used to introduce caring, sheltering and feeding for a forthcoming general-interest series broadcast.

As the spring term progressed, the activities associated with the general interest series took precedence over the language series. Mrs A felt the children were responding to, and enjoying, the general-interest series more than the language series. She believed that the events in the programmes referred more specifically to the children, and the open-endedness of the programmes gave her greater

41

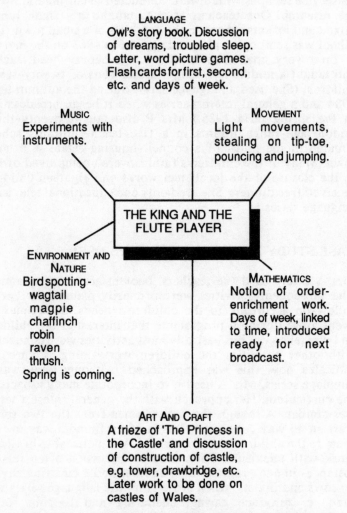

LANGUAGE
Owl's story book. Discussion of dreams, troubled sleep. Letter, word picture games. Flash cards for first, second, etc. and days of week.

MUSIC
Experiments with instruments.

MOVEMENT
Light movements, stealing on tip-toe, pouncing and jumping.

THE KING AND THE FLUTE PLAYER

ENVIRONMENT AND NATURE
Bird spotting -
wagtail
magpie
chaffinch
robin
raven
thrush.
Spring is coming.

MATHEMATICS
Notion of order-enrichment work. Days of week, linked to time, introduced ready for next broadcast.

ART AND CRAFT
A frieze of 'The Princess in the Castle' and discussion of construction of castle, e.g. tower, drawbridge, etc. Later work to be done on castles of Wales.

Figure 3.1 An example of how a teacher incorporated an off-air educational television programme with other activities

opportunity to integrate them with ongoing activities. She reported that the children were very interested as they were able to relate the physical activities they participated in, e.g. dancing, swimming, judo, etc, to the television series. A great deal of activity appeared to result from using the series in all aspects of the curriculum.

A Teacher's Summary of Use of Educational Television

From the accounts given, and from witnessing events in the classroom, Mrs A was making effective use of television. She summarized her views on the medium by saying:

Selectivity is necessary when children view television in general. In particular, educational programmes for young children should be stimulating and thought-provoking, and be a basis for further experience, exploration and extension of interest. There should always be preparation before, and follow-on activities for maximum effect.

This being the criteria, educational television can bring enrichment experiences into the classroom, in that it can stimulate thought, creativity, imagination and language through active viewing. It is not a teacher replacement, but a multi-media, audio-visual aid for the teacher's use, and the viewing should be a shared experience so that the teacher can gauge the children's responses.

Selection of material

When selecting educational television material, I consider the following points:

1   Is it suitable for the age-group viewing? (Unless it is linked to the children's experience much information is lost.)
2   Is the quality and level of language suitable?
3   Is the presentation and organization of material adequate?
4   Is it relevant to the children's ongoing experiences?
5   Does it link with schemes of work ongoing in the classroom?
6   Is it an additional desirable learning experience?
7   Does it bring enrichment experiences into the classroom?

In order for the programme to be effective and to further children's experiences, I try to be aware of the programme content beforehand. Therefore, before the television programme the children and I have discussions and activities that, hopefully, heighten interest and provide motivation and experiences. The children are encouraged to talk about the programme and eventually recognize the purposes of seeing it.

Follow-on activities

I organize follow-on activities and discussion, and prepare work to correlate with seasonal activities, reading and mathematics schemes and/or activities arising as a result of the children's particular interests in the programme. It is good if a linking theme between weekly programmes is thought out, either through use of a video recorder if one is available, or the use of the programme booklet, which gives a synopsis of the content and time for discussions and craft work, etc.

One can see that the use of the video recorder could be a tremendous advantage in being able to work out the educational content of a school television broadcast before presentation to the children.

Values of television

I feel that the value of a good television programme as an educational aid is that it is a familiar medium, which can give enjoyment through interest. It broadens a child's interests, and so extends the immediate environment. It stimulates imagination and interest and develops artistic ideas, so that the information presented, and reinforced by the teacher, may be retained over a longer period.

There should be an increased vocabulary and understanding of words, with social development and relationships enhanced through discussion and expression of ideas. A programme may have a calming effect or it may give emotional release.

Sitting, looking, listening, and concentrating is a means of self-discipline and, although my aim is for active not passive viewers, if prior activities have been well carried out, the interest in the programme is such that the children are stimulated to be attentive.

CASE STUDY B

Mrs B divided her class into four groups that were assigned a particular study skill for one hour a day. An integrated day operated for the rest of the time with individual, group, and class activities taking place. The reading and mathematics programmes were structured but creative writing was left to the individual child with the teacher making only a few suggestions. The children chose their own occupation for a large part of the day so follow-on work from educational television was largely initiated by them and not by the teacher. The children were taken as a class to a spare room, which had a carpeted area and curtains, to watch television.

Integration into Classroom Work

Mrs B regarded television as a supplement to her teaching and the sound of the week from the language series was incorporated into the structure of her reading programme. It was introduced into the children's activities a few days before the broadcast. Other activities such as making a frieze or explaining something which would feature in the programme were undertaken. On the whole, Mrs B regarded the story in the programme as a bonus to the particular sound dealt with in the programme. Nevertheless, Mrs B also sought opportunities for the children to follow on in other areas of the curriculum. Mrs B made the following observations on the use of educational television:

> The way in which a teacher uses an educational television programme depends on her 'style' of teaching - how the class is organized, whether she prefers class teaching to individual work and how she believes that learning occurs.

Organizing for viewing TV programme

It is best for one class with one teacher to watch the programme if this can be arranged. Other classes distract by coming in late and other teachers use the programme in a different way, perhaps asking questions of the children or pointing out details during the broadcast.

The best position for the teacher to sit when viewing is on a small chair at the side of the class. This is a convenient position in which to control the use of the television set and it also enables her to share the programme with the children and observe their reactions.

Use of the programme

Infants' schools have always something special taking place - festivals, assemblies, open-days, projects, seasonal studies, visitors, etc. and the television programme can seem like an intrusion into the school day. If a teacher feels that she has to use the programme as a starting point as the booklet implies she can feel very guilty if she is not able to do so. There seem to be three ways in which the programme can validly be used:

1 As a starting point;
2 To tie in with existing activities;
3 For enjoyment, with the teacher or children selecting relevant material to foster new work or to fit in with existing schemes on a class or individual basis, i.e. incorporating 1 and 2.

She made the following comments about the value of the story and the teachers' booklet:

The story

This is probably the most valuable part of each programme and the children invariably enjoy it. There appear to be two types of story shown:

1 *Stories told for practice in reading* The plot of these is usually simple and the story may be well-known. The 'Tale of a Turnip', for example, introduced each character separately by picture and word. These were then added to the story as each sentence appeared. The children knew the words as they appeared and they read them. If these words can be related to the words in the reading scheme used in the school and/or the book is available in the classroom, the television story could be an invaluable part of the curriculum.
2 *Stories told to extend vocabulary* These stories do not require a written display and when it is provided it detracts from the words used in the story as the children have to struggle to read it. More involved

plots could be attempted if the written display was not obligatory.

The teachers' booklet

The booklet as it stands is useful as a resource book for things to do at a later date. The most useful type of booklet would be one which could be made into a loose-leaf book. Each programme would occupy both sides of a page and would contain details of all of the content with songs, information about techniques and books used, etc. added. Pictures and pages to cut up to make the apparatus suggested in the programme could be provided at the end of the booklet and the whole could be incorporated into a file to be used when required. This type of booklet would be even more valuable when a school obtained a video recorder.

SUMMARY

Although both teachers used different types of teaching there were certain views they both held and taught accordingly.

1   Both indicate that judicious use can be made of off-air broadcasts if a teacher is willing, and prepared, to consider the possibilities of how they might be incorporated into ongoing activities.
2   Both accepted that a teacher needs to give a great deal of thought to planning and for the teachers' booklet to provide adequate details of what a programme will contain.
3   Neither teacher allowed a programme to direct her teaching.
4   Both teachers used a language series as a stimulus and to supplement what they intended for the children. This is contrary to the finding of Choat *et al.* (1987) who contended that most teachers used the series primarily to foster language and reading skills by direct follow-up from programmes.
5   Both teachers showed that a language series need not be confined solely to language teaching but the content used to stimulate other areas of the curriculum.
6   Mrs B stressed the importance of the story. Although Mrs A did not put the same emphasis on this as Mrs B

she also thought the story important.
7   They both contemplated what they might achieve with a video recorder. Mrs A had persuaded her headteacher to purchase a video recorder. This had just arrived at the school and she was looking forward to explore the use of this facility. Mrs B was reluctant to change her present system. She believed that the element of surprise would be lost with a video recorder.

REFERENCE

Choat, E., Griffin, H., and Hobart, D. (1987) *Teachers and Television* Beckenham: Croom Helm.

Chapter Four

USE OF THE VIDEO RECORDER

DIRECT TEACHING FROM TELEVISION

There is a body of opinion, which is mostly American, that children can learn directly from television. Most of this opinion is centred around the series *Sesame Street* and *The Electric Company*. These programmes are orientated toward skill acquisition and Williams (1981) agrees that there is some evidence that children can learn from them. Solomon (1976), commenting on the importation of *Sesame Street* into Israel, stated that the overall effect was clear; although there were social-class and age differences all age groups learned what the series designers declared it was intended to teach them. However, only seven and eight year olds showed improved skill mastery; five year olds, even when heavily exposed to the series, did not show any improvement in skill mastery and were far below the seven and eight year olds in their comprehension level. No teachers in our survey used the programme and they indicated that they did not want to teach in this way. However, there is a need for more research in this area.

LEARNING FROM TELEVISION

Because of the lack of research, especially with young children it is difficult to say what children actually learn from a continuous educational television programme.

Children looking at television are not really processing the information portrayed. Many adults assume that children are interpreting from television as they do themselves, but this is a mistaken premise. It does appear that children are increasingly able to focus on central information as thought processes develop. Collins, Wellman, Keniston, and Westby

(1978) indicated increasing attention to content central to a plot throughout the primary years. Williams (1981) stated that whatever the theoretical perspective, it is clear that much of what is portrayed on the television screen is not understood by young children. He acknowledged an increase in learning of both central and peripheral matters up to adolescence, but emphasized that there had been very few studies of children under the age of about eight years.

STUDIES OF CHILDREN'S LEARNING

These views were given some confirmation from a small study which we carried out (Choat and Griffin 1986a). Top infant children were tested for their comprehension on a 'Canals' broadcast in a general interest series. This programme was shown continuously by video playback to groups of five or six children who were then questioned individually afterwards. Most of the children were unable to make any logical interpretation from what they had seen on the tape. Their responses were isolated impressions, often removed from the basis of the programme. They had not acquired any understanding of canal boat life or realized the importance of canals. Most of them referred to narrow boats as canals and, in fact, they had the impression that the programme was about boats and how to make a model boat. The presenters' description of how canals were constructed was lost on the children.

This implies that not only has programme content to be interpreted but also the presenter's language which is meaningless unless the children's prior experiences are related to what is being discussed. The children emerged from their passive state only when they were attracted by isolated aspects or by an event which they liked and most of these were unrelated to the programme theme. Something extraordinary or stimulating had to happen for the children's attention to be held for a period of time. This occurred with a sequence when a narrow boat was legged through a tunnel, which led to a great deal of fantasy and imagination.

These findings were confirmed by a further small study which we undertook, again with top infants (Choat and Griffin 1986b). The children were split into three groups and each week, over a ten-week period, a story was read to Group A and the same story was seen on television by Groups B and C. Whereas Group B was prepared for the story, and appropriate questions using stop/start video during transmission, no such interaction took place with Group C who merely watched the story on television. All of the children were tested for their comprehension of the first and last of ten stories. The largest gains in comprehension were made by Group B where the story had been interpreted and rationalized by the teacher. They were also able to give better alternative endings to the story. Both television groups remembered the facts of a story better than the group who had been told the story by the teacher. Providing a story is suitable for the child's level of development, it does seem to have a greater impact when seen on television, probably because of the visual presentation, and this seems to aid children's memory. A detailed account of research into children's learning using educational television is given in Chapter 1 of *Teachers and Television* (Choat *et al*. 1987).

DISADVANTAGES OF OFF-AIR VIEWING

When using off-air viewing, continuous viewing of a programme has to take place. However, when a teacher has use of a video recorder she is able to stop/start and freeze-frame the video tape and this gives more effective use. Bates (1984) summarized this as follows:

> The use of cassettes has clearly revealed the limitation of broadcast television in comparison to cassettes. Broadcasts are ephemeral, cannot be interrupted or stopped, are single paced, self contained and dense in information, in the terms available for processing.
>
> Cassettes on the other hand, can be stopped while activities and discussions take place, can be reviewed segment by segment, and can be structured in a wider variety of ways than broadcasts. Cassettes give teachers and learners greater control, can be used for mastery learning, reflection, analysis, interrogation of evidence and more individual learning. To summarize, broadcasting is a weak instructional medium compared with cassettes.

While Bates was referring more to adults and older children when he made the above remarks, it probably applies equally if not more so to younger children, who find difficulty in comprehending material shown on television.

We are in agreement with Bates and were very disappointed that only a very small number of teachers in our survey used the video recorder in any other way than being able to see programmes at suitable times.

USE OF THE VIDEO RECORDER

Because we believe that effective use of the video recorder could make a very important advance in the use of educational television, the remainder of this chapter will explain the use of the video recorder and the next three chapters will deal with its use in schools and the conditions necessary to be able to use it to its full effect. It is expected that in the next few years, almost every primary school will possess at least one video recorder.

ADVANTAGES OF VIDEO RECORDERS

1 *Timetable convenience* Programmes can be shown at a time that suits the teacher
2 *Previewing* Programmes can be seen by the teacher before they are seen by the children.
3 *Use of video recorder control* Sequences can be stopped or started at an appropriate juncture for interaction between teacher and children. A particular frame can be frozen to act as a still picture. The rewind mechanism allows a return to a particular sequence for clarification or repetition and the fast forward control permits aspects not required to be by-passed.
4 *Group and individual work* The use of group work is facilitated and children can also use the video recorder individually.
5 *Resource libraries* Schools can build up resource libraries and/or can use resource centres provided by the Authorities.
6 *Purchase of tapes* Tapes can be purchased that are produced by the broadcasting companies or other agencies.

Timetable Convenience

This is when children still view together by class or mass viewing. An off-air broadcast is played back at a time which suits the teacher. This does not interrupt assembly, singing, PE, etc., if the class is timetabled for those activities at a time when a programme is transmitted. The playback is continuous from the beginning to the end of a programme and not stopped at any point. One teacher interviewed in the pilot year used this in a different way. She wished to view a series of programmes, but because a large number of schools in the area were using the same series she was not able to obtain the visual aids she required. The programmes were recorded and used the next term when the materials were available. Timetable convenience is by far the most widespread form of video recorder use at present.

Previewing

There were very few examples of teachers previewing in our survey. Most teachers claimed that a teacher in an infant school had very little time for this. While this is certainly true the main reason seemed to be that the vast majority of teachers viewed programmes continuously and did not really see the need to preview programmes beforehand. They believed they could rely on the programme notes or previous knowledge of a series to decide whether it was worth seeing. One teacher, who had special responsibility for audio-visual aids in the school, recorded a series of programmes, decided they were unsuitable for the children and recommended the other teachers in the school should not view them. Another teacher recorded ten programmes in a new series for viewing in the following terms, but only viewed two or three because the rest were thought unsuitable. If more programmes were previewed it is probable that more decisions of this kind would be taken and time saved which could be used for other purposes.

One of the small group of teachers who made effective use of video controls first viewed the programme off-air with the children and then followed up later using the video facilities. Apart from saving time she claimed that this was an advantageous way in which to use the recorder. The way programmes are at present made there is an advantage in seeing programmes continuously. The teacher claimed that from this first viewing she could decide which parts of the programme needed to be explained in more detail, although this could be modified by the children's responses. Some programmes were not considered of sufficient value to be dealt with in any more detail, but it must be questioned whether these programmes should have been shown originally.

Use of Video Controls

This is the most important function of the video recorder.

Instead of playing through continuously the teacher is able to intervene and bring the children into the proceedings rather than having them watch passively. The playback may be in progress for only a minute or even less before the teacher wishes the children to interact and she repeats the process as many times as she wishes. Furthermore the children are able to ask for the tape to be stopped or played back for something they wished to see again. However, there are some difficulties when teachers first start to use the recorder in this way, and we suggest that they should proceed in two stages.

Basic stop/start

This method of operation differs little from off-air viewing. Whole-class or mass viewing is still practised. A teacher may occasionally stop the video recorder to get the children to read a caption or point something out. The children are not given the opportunity to interact with the playback or with the teacher and are expected to behave passively. Previewing is not absolutely necessary when using this method. Although this method has only a slight advantage over off-air viewing it does give the teacher practice in using the controls and it is hoped that she would gain sufficient confidence to proceed to the next stage.

Secondary stop/start

A completely different format emerges when this stage is completed. The teacher could either preview the programme or see the programme with the children as illustrated in the section on previewing. Children are encouraged to participate and are actively involved rather than being expected to view passively. Teachers would probably reach full and effective use by a number of steps:

1 If they were mass viewing they would change to class viewing.
2 Stops would be made at definite points in the programme. The contents would be discussed with the children at these points.
3 Tape would be run back to illustrate certain points and further discussion would take place.
4 Children would be allowed to interrupt at any point and the tape would be stopped, started and run back

and forward as appropriate.
5   Teachers would change to group viewing as this would facilitate discussion and allow more children to participate.

Teachers were observed during the second year at various stages of development and examples will be given in the following chapters. Although these stages took different times to reach, according to the confidence and ability of the teacher, all teachers who had reached a certain stage found no problems in operating at that level.

Group Work

Most teachers in our discussion groups did not think it was possible to use television in small groups. We have had similar responses at courses and conferences that we have attended. The immediate response is that it is not possible with a class of thirty children because of the disturbance to other children. However, it has been demonstrated by a few teachers that a small group of children for whom a programme or part of a programme is relevant can be withdrawn from the other children. This procedure may take a few weeks to initiate but once children become accustomed to the practice it becomes an accepted part of the school day. They continue with their activities while not watching, knowing their turn will come to watch television later. Our evidence confirms that children are not distracted at what is going on in a corner of the classroom. They happily continue with what they are doing. After all, teachers devise group work for other activities that they carry out in the classroom, so why should television be different?
From observations in the classroom we are quite convinced that secondary stop/start techniques vastly improve the teachers' effectiveness in using television. This is further emphasized when children are taught in groups rather than taught in a class. Teachers found the use of a remote control helpful: they could choose the position they wished to operate from when the children were viewing.

Individual Interaction

Using the video recorder is not beyond the capabilities of the majority of primary school children. However, if a child needs to learn in this way, material must be very carefully prepared by the teacher, and this would be very time-consuming. Only one teacher we observed in our groups allowed children to use television in this way and this will be reported in a later chapter. Even teachers who used group work very effectively did not feel that they wished to cater for children in this way, although they recognized the possibilities. Probably, we would need commercially produced programmes before this becomes a practical possibility for most teachers.

Resources

Possession of a video recorder allows schools to build up a collection of video tapes. There are some problems with the copyright laws, but legislation at present going through Parliament means that most of the problems will probably be resolved before this book is published. Most schools in our survey had a small collection of tapes. These were usually programmes that a school had found useful and wished to use in the next year or subsequent years when they would probably not be broadcast. In only two of the schools in the survey had they sufficient tapes that teachers could use if they wished to plan the curriculum using television resource material. These two schools were visited in the second year of the research and the advantages of a resource library in schools will be discussed in the next chapter. However, the conclusion we came to was that resource libraries in school are very valuable, but a great deal of time and money needs to be spent to make them a success. Most primary schools will need to rely on local authority resource centres. Three of these were visited and their usefulness will be reported on in a later chapter.

Purchase of tapes

Tapes produced by the broadcasting companies and commercial agencies can be purchased for use with video recorders and would be of great value to schools. We have produced tapes which could be used in primary schools and details of these and reasons for production will be given in a later chapter. The problem is that primary schools may not have sufficient money and may have to rely on resources provided by local centres.

IN-SERVICE AND PRE-SERVICE EDUCATION

The following three chapters will give examples of what can be achieved by teachers who are interested and willing to use television effectively, and are in schools with adequate resources. However, most teachers can improve their teaching using television providing they consider it to be of importance. For this they need more help from inspectors and advisers and provision of in-service education. This would be facilitated if more emphasis was given to television and the use of video recorders in initial training.

REFERENCES

Bates, A.W. (1984) 'Splitting image', *The Times Educational Supplement*, 2/4/84.

Choat, E. and Griffin, H. (1986a) 'Young children, television and learning, Part 1, The effects of children watching a continuous off-air broadcast', *Journal of Educational Television* 12: 79-89.

Choat, E., Griffin, H., (1986b) 'Young children, television and learning Pt. II, Comparison of the effects of reading and story telling by the teacher and television story viewing', *Journal of Educational Television* 13:9104.

Choat, E., Griffin, H. and Hobart, D. (1986) *Teachers and Television*, Beckenham: Croom Helm.

Collins, W.A., Wellman, H., Kenniston, A.H., and Westby, S.D. (1978) 'Age related aspects of comprehension and interference from a televised dramatic narrative', *Child Development*, 49:389-99.

Solomon, G. (1976) 'Sesame Street around the World: cognitive skill learning across the cultures', *Journal of Communication* 26:138-44.

Williams, T.M. (1981) 'How and what do children learn from television?', *Human Communication Research* 7: 180-92.

Chapter Five

EXAMPLES IN THE USE OF THE VIDEO RECORDER IN SCHOOLS

About a third of the teachers in our research (Choat *et al.* 1987) had access to a video recorder. This compared with the estimated 40 per cent of schools that had video recorders in England and Wales as a whole at that time. Moss (1987) reported that 72 per cent of primary schools in England and Wales possessed a video recorder at the time he was writing. Ways of using the video recorder were discussed in the last chapter. In our survey schools simply used video recorders for the purpose of timetable convenience and programmes were viewed in a similar way to off-air broadcasts. However, there were a few teachers who did use the video recorders in more imaginative ways and a few also changed during the period of the project. Some of these teachers were observed and interviewed in the schools and this chapter is devoted to the examples of their practice together with a discussion of some of the changes which are required in schools to enable the video recorder to be used to its full potential.

CASE STUDY DETAILS

Three schools were visited for this purpose. Two of these were situated in an urban Merseyside fringe area and although the schools were a few miles apart the children came from similar social-economic areas. There was only a small number of children whose parents were not born in Britain and although there were a few parents who were unemployed this was very small compared with some inner-city areas nearby. The schools' educational standards were a little higher than would normally be expected from children of this age. Both schools maintained good relationships and received lots of help from the parents.

SCHOOL A

The first school was an infant school with six classes, which had increased to seven by the final visit. All the original teachers had been very co-operative members of the survey group. They attended all in-service sessions connected with the project, except when illness or unavoidable commitments prevented this. All questionnaires and pro formas were conscientiously completed even though, at times, this required a lot of extra work on their part. Visits were made to the second school during the autumn and spring terms 1984/85 and again in the summer term 1987.

Provision of Facilities

The headteacher, who had been a research group leader, was very keen to promote the effective use of television. In 1983 she began recording all the infant school educational television series, using a different tape for each series. Unfortunately, as she only had the use of one video recorder, it was not possible to make effective use of the timing mechanism and the recording involved her in a great deal of time and inconvenience. She thought that to operate the system effectively she needed another recorder and television receiver which could be placed on a trolley and used in any classroom where teachers required it. Details of how this system can be used effectively will be given later in the chapter. Parents had purchased the first video recorder, and when the last visit was made they had also purchased a second. She had not, however, mastered the technique of back to back recording (transfers from one recorder to another), but hoped she would be able to do this in the next academic year.

Initial Visits

During the 1984/85 visits the teachers were sceptical about the traditional use of educational television and were giving a lot of thought to how it could be used more effectively. There were six teachers in the school, two in each age range and co-operative teaching was encouraged. The two teachers in the top age group were making effective use of the resource library available in the school. A mathematics series had been found useful in a previous year. This had been recorded and more effective use was made of the programmes in the following year. It was not necessary to see all of the programmes or view them in any special order. In fact, they were used when it was most suitable for the majority of the class, and even parts of the programme were used if this was thought to be appropriate. It was suggested that this could be used by small groups of children, but the teachers considered this would cause too many problems. They thought it would be a good idea if they could set up a resource library covering different mathematical notions which could be suitable for all children in the schools. This request has been supported by a number of teachers (Choat *et al.* 1987). For the summer term they had planned a topic on Water which included visits and covered work in all curriculum areas. They intended to use a number of suitable tapes which were in the resource area. This was a use of resources that was rarely encountered in the survey. Little use was made of stop/start techniques, as the teachers thought older children liked to see programmes from beginning to end. The teachers considered there was very little value in viewing the same television series every week.

The two teachers in the second year used the television in more traditional ways. Two classes viewed a language series but they did use a basic stop/start technique so children were able to read the words on the screen. Follow-up procedure was carried out under fairly traditional lines. While there is some value in the basic stop/start technique it was hoped that this approach would give teachers experience so that they would use the stop/start techniques in more imaginative ways. However, they had not changed when they were visited six months later and saw no reason why change was required.

Final Visits

When these two teachers were last visited, one was working with a reception class while the other was teaching an older age group and they used a team teaching approach, working with two different teachers. The teacher with the reception class had not changed her views, and rarely used television because she claimed that series for this age group were not suitable. The other teacher had changed her views. She thought there was an advantage in using meaningful stop/start and had experimented in teaching with small groups. There was very good co-operation with the other teacher in the team who had similar views on the use of television. Neither of the teachers used the traditional form of viewing of following up a set programme but used the schools resource library when this fitted in with the work they were doing with the class. They stated they did not use the resources sufficiently and needed to plan a topic more carefully if they were to take advantage of the resources now available. There were problems because they liked topics to arise from children's interests, but claimed they could overcome this difficulty if they planned carefully. A wallchart produced by the IBA, which is now printed annually, could be of great help to them.

Both the teachers in the teams agreed that teaching was more effective when a secondary stop/start technique was used, especially if teaching was in small groups, the method they usually used. They both possessed video recorders at home and saw programmes which could have assisted them in their teaching. At present they are restricted in this use because of copyright laws. There is proposed Parliamentary legislation which will allow teachers to use video in this way and a number of teachers would probably take advantage of this. It is hoped that the bill which was put back because of the last General Election will not be delayed too long.

Secondary Stop/Start Techniques and Need for Previewing

In the first series of visits one teacher was observed teaching the reception class. She tended to do a fair amount of teaching to the whole class although the children's work was carried out individually or in groups. Only one general interest series was used as she thought that this was sufficient time to spend on television. She was very enthusiastic about the use of stop/start techniques and could not understand why this was not used by all teachers. There was no doubt in her mind that educational television was far more effective when used this way. The children could join in the programme and discussion and questioning could be used to great advantage.

Language development was the main purpose of the teaching and she claimed this could be used effectively even with children who had just entered school. Any series would be suitable providing it related to the children's experience. On the two occasions she was observed, her claims seemed fully justified. Even though she had not previewed the programmes, it did seem as though she was teaching what she had prepared and the television was being used as an aid to her teaching. Sometimes this would be followed up and some interesting work obtained from the children. She claimed that there was no suitable topic work series for children of her age group, but did not really require one as topic work should arise from the children's interests. Occasionally programmes had been used from the school's resource library and she would have used this facility more often if she had been able to have a television in the classroom.

This teacher was visited again when she was using a language series on a regular basis with a second-year infants' group. She did follow up with some of the suggestions in the teachers' notes, but only with a group of children who might gain advantage from the use of the suggestions. Because she was able to use a photocopier in school, this follow-up work could be easily prepared. Some of the programmes were not suitable for the secondary stop/start technique and not a lot of value could be obtained from them. She was observed viewing a programme that emphasized this. The programme was only stopped on a couple of occasions and the children did not appear to gain a great deal from viewing.

Although this teacher does not feel that previewing programmes is necessary it would enable her not to show programmes that she would recognize as being of little value. While it would not be easy with this teacher's style of teaching to make much use of the resource library to the full effect, she could use small groups to advantage. A small group using a suitable programme would gain immensely from a skilled teacher using secondary stop/start techniques.

Summary - School A

1   This school under the guidance of an enthusiastic headteacher had made very good progress in the use of educational television.

2   They were gradually building up a school resource library and this growth should be accelerated as use was made of the second video recorder.

3   Two of the teachers were making excellent use of facilities and using small group teaching and stop/start techniques very effectively. They were still not using resource material to its full effect but expected to do so when more resource material was available. At the beginning of the project both teachers had been using television in fairly conventional ways.

4   Two of the teachers no longer used television in traditional ways. They made good use of the school resource library and had planned topics using these resources. Although they had both previously used mathematics series, they now only used programmes when appropriate. However,

they rarely used stop/start techniques and when they did it was only at a basic level. They thought it was not practical to use small group viewing even though there were examples of its use in the school.

5 One teacher had been using stop/start techniques effectively since the beginning of the project. Unfortunately she had made little change in her methods and did not see the need for previewing or small viewing. Now the second video recorder has been obtained she thought she could use this in the classroom, and make more use of resource material in topic work.

6 One teacher claimed that traditional television viewing was ineffective but had reacted by not using television in any way in her teaching.

7 All of the teachers in the school had seriously assessed the use of educational television and had made changes, even though in one instance this had meant stopping using television altogether.

8 The headteacher thought much more work needed to be done and spoke about the need for in-service and pre-service training.

9 The headteacher and staff thought it necessary that local provision should be made for the supply of resource material.

SCHOOL B

The other school visited in the area was a junior mixed and infant school which had eight junior and five infants' classes. Only three of the infants' teachers took part in the initial research, and they were the only teachers together with a teacher responsible for audio-visual aids who were interviewed on the initial visits.

Resource Library and Use of Small-Group Teaching

The head teacher firmly believed that it was possible to provide a resource library in the school and if teachers used this effectively small-group teaching using secondary stop/start techniques should be the common practice for all teachers. They had two televisions and two video recorders in the school. The second recorder and receiver were placed on a mobile trolley and it was intended that this would be used by small groups in the classroom. The first recorder and receiver remained static and was used for recording purposes or for teachers who still wanted to use an off-air broadcast.

Initially, the headteacher thought there would be some intrusion into the normal teaching climate as groups sat around the TV/video unit, just as there was when computers were introduced into the classroom, but the intrusion should be short-lived. The key was to have fairly frequent use made of the unit, as once it is accepted as a commonplace addition to the furniture of the room, it is soon ignored except by those making use of it. Fortunately, the school is all on one level and it is not difficult to move the mobile unit from room to room.

Organization of Resource Library and Role of Co-ordinator for Audio-Visual Aids

For the above system to operate effectively, it is necessary that sufficient resources are provided. This was the responsibility of the junior school teacher responsible for visual aids who was a science graduate and had received training in the use of audio-visual aids. Apart from the above responsibility he was co-ordinator for the teaching of science and technology in the school. He seemed a very keen and conscientious person. The mechanics of the recording, storing, and cataloguing of tapes he did not find particularly difficult. He would set the recorder each morning to record the programmes that were required for the day. Each Friday he would transfer programmes by means of back-to-back recording on a tape for that particular series. It was just possible to record a term's programmes on one 3-hour tape and all tapes would be catalogued as shown in Table 5.1

The completed cassette would be placed in the resource library at the end of the term, but could be used during the term it was being recorded if requested. All teachers' booklets of the series were obtained and these were placed alongside the tapes. At the end of the year a full catalogue of tapes was printed so that teachers were aware of all the tapes that were available. The teacher thought it would be more efficient if thirty-minute tapes containing one or two programmes were recorded but this would cause a big increase in cost. The recording and cataloguing took about three to four hours a week, but some time was also spent in ensuring that audio and video equipment was in good working order, and arranging for the use of the mobile unit if this was required in more than one place at one time. He was kept very busy especially as his other school duties needed to be carried out.

Table 5.1 An example of how programmes were categorized by a teacher

Middle English Count numbers	Volume Four	Age Range: Upper Juniors Title of programme
000		The Making of Zulu Dawn
259		Izzy Part 1
464		Izzy Part 2
645		Diaries
804		Punctuation
964		Middle Pages – Story teller
1,098		News of War
1,258		A Game of Soldiers Part 1
1,373		A Game of Soldiers Part 2
1,480		A Game of Soldiers Part 3

This teacher was of the opinion that there was no need to arrange material under topic headings which some teachers may find useful. Teachers could do this themselves, especially with the help of the previously mentioned annual IBA wall chart which teachers in this school did use. He agreed it would be a great advantage if mathematics topics could be edited and catalogued under different mathematical notions but did not think this could be done in the school, because of the amount of work involved.

The IBA produced a very useful book which discussed the use of the video recorder in school. It was suggested in this book that there should be a more sophisticated method of storage and evaluation of recorded material than was practised in this particular school. It was suggested that a card should be made for each programme which teachers could use to make a programme evaluation. This would be important to other teachers who used the programme and would help in making decisions about whether it was necessary to retain the programme for future years. It would also be helpful when copyright laws allow programmes to be used in the classroom that are not specifically produced for education, as there would be no teachers' notes to give an indication of the content of the programme. However, more time would need to be spent on cataloguing and editing, which the teacher concerned did not have available.

The choice of material to be taped was greatly influenced by the co-ordinator for audio-visual aids. His criteria for choice of recording was firstly what was appropriate for the child and secondly where the teacher could be helped. There was a bias in recording towards the junior age range and to mathematics and science. An analysis was made of the programmes recorded and catalogued by the end of the 1986 academic year. Table 5.2 illustrates the above points.

Table 5.2 Analysis of programmes recorded and catalogued in the school

Prog-rammes	Maths	Science	English	General interest	Health education	Total
Infants	29	-	-	-	5	34
Junior	79	51	47	34	5	216
	108	51	47	34	10	250

The above programmes had been recorded on 29 tapes. However, during the 1986/87 year there had been a demand for tapes in the infants' school and a number of general interest programmes had been recorded which had made a significant increase available in the stock of programmes suitable for infants.

Use of Video Recorder on First Visit

The amount of programmes available was obviously reflected in the use of the video recorder in the school. On the first visit to the school only three infant teachers, who were members of the research group, were interviewed about their classroom practice. At this time only mathematics programmes were available on tape. They claimed that the mathematics series was very useful. One teacher said it was an introduction to numbers for the young children and a reinforcement for the brighter children. The use of stop/start techniques was particularly valuable for this series. On the first visit the teachers were asked why they did not adopt small-group viewing, even though some resources were available and the head teacher encouraged this. They realized that they would probably try this before the next visit when the children had become more accustomed to the routine. On the next visit the views of the two remaining staff were similar but they had not materially altered their techniques. They stated that there was a shortage of suitable series for young children for group viewing, but saw no reason why this could not be used with mathematics series.

The headteacher was aware that the teachers were not using the programmes in the ways suggested, even though five of the eight junior teachers were using television for group viewing, and incorporating it in the curriculum. He did accept that it was more difficult for teachers in the reception class because of the lack of suitable material, and the children's immaturity. Group teaching was, however, most important in infants' classes and he saw no reason why the use of television could not be part of the curriculum and approached with this aim in view. He was anxious to discuss further teaching methods in general with the infant section, and how the use of television could be best incorporated into the curriculum.

Use of Video Recorder on the Final Visit (Infant Teachers)

On the final visit there was evidence of considerable change in the infant section of the school. Two of the teachers in a team-teaching situation in the first year made excellent use of video material. They adopted an approach that relied mainly on group and individual teaching and there was very good co-operation between the teachers. Whenever television was required this was fitted into the curriculum. Secondary stop/start techniques were the common practice. When the children first started school it took about half a term before they had really become accustomed to the use of television in small groups, but, as the teachers pointed out, there were similar problems when the microcomputer was first introduced. They used a mathematics series which they found useful, but claimed there were too many mathematical notions introduced in one programme. Secondary stop/start techniques did make it more effective to use, but they, in common with many other teachers in our survey group, would like video tapes dealing with one mathematical notion.

There were occasional problems when the mobile video unit was not available but the teachers claimed that their teaching was flexible enough to cope with this. They had tried making a timetable for its use but this had not proved as successful as arranging this by mutual agreement, with a little help and persuasion from the co-ordinator for visual aids. The headteacher saw there could be problems when teachers used small-group teaching more extensively and hoped to provide a second mobile video as soon as possible. Because of the enthusiasm of teachers in the teams, a wider variety of video tapes suitable for infants' schools had been recorded and were available in the resource centre.

Use of Video Recorders in Junior Schools

One teacher in the junior school had very similar views to those of the infants' school teachers. Her views on the production of videos for the teaching of mathematical notions were similar, although she thought that some of the present mathematics programmes for juniors could be used quite effectively in groups. Because her children were older and had some experience with television they were able to adapt to using video recordings with small groups without any problems. She did watch one programme off-air which was very unusual in this school. This was a music series, an area in which she was not competent. There was some specialized music teaching in the school, but the series reinforced this. She particularly liked the presentation because the children worked in groups at the direction of the presenter.

All teachers in the junior school seemed to accept these views of educational television. Their enthusiasm for its use obviously varied, and it was used in different ways according to their particular teaching style and interests. However, they had given thought to its use and had rejected the idea that television could only be used in the traditional ways practised by most teachers. They were fortunate, of course, in having such an extensive resource library.

Summary - School B

1   This school was more advanced than any other school in the project and had been since the beginning of the project.
2   Most of the teachers in the school used group teaching and secondary stop/start techniques, and found no particular difficulty in doing this.
3   This was one of two schools in the project which had a very good school resource library. The headteacher in the school was very dynamic and committed to the use of

audio-visual aids. He had appointed a teacher responsible for these who supported the headteacher and had organized a very efficient system which he and the headteacher encouraged teachers to use.

4   The biggest change during the time of the project had been the change of attitude in the infant school. Although they had been influenced by taking part in the project, the change had been mainly brought about by the influence of the headteacher and the judicious transfer of a junior teacher to the infant section, who had influenced the other teachers by her use of the video recorder.

SCHOOL C

Only one other school used in our research had an extensive resource library. This was in a junior mixed and infants school in a semirural area in North Wales, with four junior classes, three infants' classes and a nursery class. There was a parent-teacher association and parents helped in the school. The three infant teachers who took part in the survey, and the headteacher, who was chairman of the research group, were interviewed. Interviews were carried out during 1984/85 with the three infant teachers and the headteacher, but there was no follow-up visit in 1987 as in the previous schools reported.

School resources

The headmaster, who was born and still lives in the area, was very enthusiastic about all work involving the use of audio-visual aids. Apart from video material he had a large collection of audio tapes, film strips and other material. All the tapes had been catalogued and were available for use by any teacher. Cataloguing had been done in a similar way to that used in the previous school but he also had a number of tapes which he had edited. Some of these covered particular themes of work.

This had involved an enormous amount of work and it is only a dedicated person who could have produced a library as extensive as the one in the school. During the time the school was visited he had become involved with the local resource centre and had co-operated with the centre to make a video tape to show the benefits of using the video recorder in more enterprising ways. The centre, reported on later, provides an excellent service and the school intended to use it to greater effect in the future. This would avoid a great deal of work and expense. However, the headteacher had produced a resource library which would be the envy of most schools and had a more comprehensive selection than the previous school.

The school had only one television receiver and recorder when the survey commenced, which meant viewing in a cloakroom area with a large television set. During the course of visits to the school the headteacher obtained a second television receiver and video recorder which had been placed on a trolley and was used by teachers when required. There were problems in moving the trolley to all classes in the school. However, as the headteacher pointed out, the provision of material and equipment does not mean it will be effectively used. Visits to the school confirmed this view.

Use of Video Recorders by Infant Teachers

The three infants' teachers had been influenced by the in-service groups run in co-operation with the research project. One teacher was very experienced and had taught a long time in the school. She had begun to use basic stop/start and found it useful. The in-service session had made her more critical of the use of educational television but as she was reaching retirement she did not think she would make any further changes in its use.

Use of Secondary Stop/Start Techniques

The second teacher had not considered stop/start techniques or making use of the school resource library before she attended the in-service sessions. During the visits she began to use the video recorder more creatively and gradually improved her stop/start techniques. She had recently started work on a transport project and in her planning had seen the value of obtaining video tapes from the local resource centre. This seemed to have worked very well and in future she intended to obtain video tapes from the local resource centre or school resource centre in a similar way to that in which she obtained other material for use in her topic work. She hoped to use this approach in other areas of the curriculum. Though not at present using television with small groups she saw the possibilities and hoped to try this way of working. The viewing area was adjacent to her classroom so she could use the large TV set when it was not required for recording purposes. It appeared as though this teacher would soon be making very effective use of the video recorder in her teaching.

The third teacher, who taught a group of rising five-year-olds made good use of the video recorder. In the autumn term when the children commenced school she let them see a series suitable for her age group. They saw the programmes live but they were all recorded. In the spring term she showed some of them again, using stop/start techniques, or even selected parts of the programme which were suitable. She also used the school resource centre extensively and previewed tapes to see which were suitable. During one of the visits she was observed making effective use of a nature tape prepared by the headteacher. The secondary stop/start technique produced a great deal of discussion from the children. The teacher thought language development was the most useful way of using television with children of the age she was teaching. She did not want to use it for topic work or mathematics. The latter, she considered, should be a practical activity for young children. If she had been teaching older children she would have integrated television work into her topic making use of the school and local resource centre. She had intended using groups in her television work, but unfortunately the nursery assistant had been absent almost since the beginning of the autumn term. When she returned, group work using video would become part of her teaching.

Summary School C

1 The three teachers in the infant school had all been influenced by taking part in the research and receiving encouragement from the headteacher.

2 One teacher had started to use secondary stop/start techniques at the beginning of the project and had improved in her use of this. She also made good use of the school resource library, although because of her views on mathematics she did not use any of the mathematics tapes with young children. She anticipated using group teaching.

3 The second teacher had used conventional teaching at the start of the project but had gradually improved her techniques. She made good use of the school resource library and had started to use the central resource library. She had not yet used group teaching but thought she would probably do so.

4 The third teacher had begun to use basic stop/start techniques, but because she was near retirement it seemed

doubtful if she would progress beyond this.
5 There was a big difference between the infant and junior departments in the schools. The junior department used television in a traditional way and the headteacher was very disappointed about this. He stressed the necessity for in-service education. Other headteachers we spoke to agreed that in-service training was essential if progress in the effective use of the video recorder was to be made.
6 Even though the headteacher had an excellent resource library, he considered that areas should have local resource centres to supply video tapes. They were fortunate that there was a very good centre in the area.

ORGANIZATION FOR THE USE OF VIDEO RECORDERS IN SCHOOLS

The three schools used for the case studies all possessed two video recorders and two television receivers. They agreed that the way to use them was to use one for recording purposes. This would remain stationary and could be used for previewing or classes who wished to watch a programme off-air. The second recorder and receiver should be placed on a mobile trolley and used in the classroom as required. One school had used them this way before the beginning of the project, and the other two schools who had just bought a second video recorder and receiver planned to use it this way.

However, a large majority of primary schools will not be so well provided and this will cause problems. Fortunately, most programmes are recorded in the morning and during this period the recorder can be used for recording programmes. Each teacher can be allocated an afternoon a week to use the video recorder for playback. This may cause problems, especially in larger schools, but it is a system that many schools adopt when using the microcomputer.

PROVISION OF VIDEO RECORDERS BY PARENT-TEACHER ASSOCIATIONS

The three schools we studied had their video recorders provided by funds from the parent-teacher association. This is common practice and, at a recent conference we organized, almost all the schools had obtained their recorder this way. Most of these schools however were in reasonably affluent areas. A number of headteachers in the poorer inner city areas did not feel justified in asking parents to contribute in this way. They also stated that with the limited amount of money they had to spend they found it very difficult to purchase one from the school capitation allowance. It does seem that extra money needs to be given to these schools to enable them to use educational television to full advantage.

REFERENCES

Choat, E., Griffin, H., and Hobart, D. (1987) *Teachers and Television*, Beckenham: Croom Helm.
Independent Broadcasting Authority (1984) *Primary and Middle School Topics*, Wallchart London: IBA.
Independent Television Companies Association (1983) *The Use of Video Recorders in School*, London: ITCA.
Moss, R. (1987) 'Thirty years on', *The Times Educational Supplement*, 8/5/87, p.36

Chapter Six

RESOURCE CENTRES, IN-SERVICE EDUCATION AND THE USE OF THE VIDEO CAMERA

While there are obvious advantages in a school having its own large resource centre, only a few schools will consider it worth while spending the time, money, and energy that this involves. Most schools which possess a video recorder will build up small collections of video tapes and will need to rely on local resource centres to provide most of the material they require if they wish to use the video recorder effectively.

Two resource centres were visited in 1985 as part of the original project on television and the curriculum, and one more has been visited recently. One of these centres was considered to be a fairly typical resource centre while the other two had been recommended as being well above average in this provision of resources. However, no general survey was made of centres and it is possible that some centres may provide better facilities than those visited, while others may provide poorer facilities than the one described as a typical centre.

The first centre visited was situated in a North Wales county town and served a large rural area.

CENTRE A - ORGANIZATION

This centre was probably the largest one of its kind. Apart from the facilities available for copying video and audio material there was a large television studio on the site and the centre had the staff and equipment to make video tapes and films of a high professional standard. The studios were so well equipped that they were rented out for part of the time to the local commercial television company.

The centre made video recordings of all programmes that schools requested in advance and could record any programme in an emergency that schools or colleges required. Copyright laws were strictly adhered to and schools broadcasts were

74

retained for three years and continuing education broadcasts for one year unless re-broadcast. Only programmes listed in the *Annual Programme for Schools and Colleges* and *Insight* programmes for continuing education were recorded. Tapes were sent out as complete programmes and no attempts were made to edit. However, programmes were categorized under different headings and printed in a booklet which all schools and colleges were able to obtain. A number of tapes were bought by the centre for distribution. They would have liked to have recorded general television programmes that teachers might think of value but this was not permitted by copyright laws. The new proposed laws on copyright may make this possible. Although the centre supplied a very wide geographical area there was a very efficient van service and all schools and colleges could be supplied weekly with audio and video material. Schools were able to purchase video recorders at reduced prices.

Availability of video tapes

In the autumn 1983 catalogue over a thousand video tapes had been listed which were recorded on VHS and there was a stock of U-Matic tapes for schools which had the equipment. In addition, eighty-three tapes had been purchased. Most tapes were 20-30 minutes in length and some contained more than one programme. When the contents of the catalogue were analysed it was found that only fifteen were suitable for infants' schools and of these eight lasted only for ten minutes.

When the small number of video tapes used by infant schools was pointed out the director claimed that this was because they were not requested by the schools in the area.

In-service education

In the discussion that ensued there were different points of view as to who should be responsible for informing infant schools on the effective use of video tapes which could lead to increased demand. There was some difficulty in this respect as this particular resource centre had no responsibility for in-service education. In co-operation with the project the centre decided to make a video tape demonstrating effective use of the video recorder in infant schools. It will be interesting to see if this has any effect in increasing the use of the facilities of the centre by infant schools in the area.

CENTRE B - ORGANIZATION

The second resource centre was situated centrally in an outer London borough. It was the curriculum development centre and was responsible for the in-service training in the area which had previously been the concern of the teachers' centre. Using the premises of a school no longer needed for teaching purposes, it was well equipped with a wide variety of teachers' material and had sufficient space to provide facilities for the provision of all the in-service courses mounted in the area. Resource material for teachers was well supplied and because of the compact nature of the area it was possible for material to be delivered to and collected from schools on a twice-weekly basis. Teachers in a school visited in the area spoke warmly of the work of the centre and were specially appreciative of the packs of material which were provided mainly for project work. Video material, however, was not provided in these project packs.

Facilities available

The centre had facilities for recording video material and recorded all the educational television programmes that were shown. This was intended as an emergency service in case a school was unable to record a programme it required. These recordings were kept for two weeks and then the tapes were re-used. This facility had been found useful on occasions, mainly by secondary schools.

The provision of more extensive services was discussed with the head of the centre and the librarian. It was agreed that the provision of video material in teachers' packs would improve the facilities offered but the centre doubted if they would have sufficient money or staff to be able to provide this on the scale required. It might be possible to improve the present facilities but this would be limited.

This type of centre seems to have the advantage over a resource centre not responsible for in-service education as help could be given in the most efficient use of video material. There are probably many centres in the country similar to this. To provide the material required for effective use of video material in school these centres would need a big increase in resources.

CENTRE C - ORGANIZATION

The third centre visited was in the West Midlands. It was part of the teachers' centre and the person in charge of the resource centre was directly responsible to the teachers' centre warden. Although no courses had been organized on the use of video resource material, this could have been arranged quite easily, if it was thought necessary.

All the primary schools in the LEA had been provided with a video recorder and they could obtain a second recorder at about a quarter of the usual cost. Many primary schools did have a stock of programmes which they had recorded. The centre had a full record of these which they circulated to all schools in the area so that schools could borrow from each other if they required a programme that they had not recorded.

Facilities Available

The centre was well stocked with 16mm films, slides, filmstrips, and wallcharts. They had also purchased over a thousand video cassettes for use in the secondary school and higher education, and over a hundred for the primary schools. However, about half of the primary tapes were storytelling tapes. Apart from these there were hardly any video tapes suitable for infants or lower juniors. Even though they had spent a lot of money purchasing tapes it was claimed that apart from the story tapes it was very difficult to buy suitable material for children of this age. The material was put together under topic headings, and would be delivered to schools on request. Deliveries and collections took place once a week.

One of the study packs contained 53 16mm films, 33 slides, 14 filmstrips, 4 teaching packs, 5 study packs, and 4 VHS video cassettes. Another pack contained 124 items of which 7 were video cassettes. Even the small number of video tapes were really only suitable for top juniors. In fact some of these were intended for the lower secondary age, but some junior schools had found them useful.

The resource centre librarian regretted the lack of video material, especially as some of the 16mm film projectors used in schools were no longer serviceable and it was difficult to do anything but minor repairs at the centre. She expected that the use of video tape material would grow as the use of 16mm film diminished.

However, in sharp contrast to the North Wales centre, no BBC or ITV school programmes were taped. The Librarian claimed that this was because of the copyright laws. Although the copyright restrictions do cause problems they are not as great as the centre leader imagined. All educational programmes for use in educational institutions may be kept for a period of three years. If the programme is broadcast again, as is usually the case, the copyright period is extended for a further three years provided the programme is re-recorded. This means a tape can be kept for six years by which time it is hoped that the copyright laws will be changed. In further discussions it transpired that the centre would need an increase in technical staff to make this possible. There was sufficient staff in the centre to classify individual tapes and place them in the appropriate project packs. It seemed as though only a small increase in technical staff was required at this centre to enable them to provide a very good video tape service for primary schools alongside the excellent provision of other audio-visual aids. However, good provision does not mean effective use. In-service courses would be needed to bring about effective use of the material.

RESOURCE SHORTAGES

Teachers in schools who are beginning to make effective use of the video recorder are often frustrated by the lack of resources available. Schools are encouraged to adopt a cross-curricular experimental approach to learning, especially when involved in topic or project work. Although many resource centres supply audio-visual material this does not often include video tapes which could be very valuable. Centre A, in our survey, was well provided but did not receive sufficient demand from the primary section. This seemed to be because of the lack of information provided by the centre or other agencies in the effective use of the material. Centre C was very well supported by the authority and blamed the operation of the copyright laws for the non-provision of programmes broadcast by the television companies. Although this can be a problem they agreed that even the present laws, which may soon be modified, allowed them to provide a much better service, though this would have needed a slight increase in technical staff. It was surprising that the head of the resource library had not co-operated with the Teachers' Centre leader, with whom she had good contact and shared the same premises, to provide courses in the effective use of the video recorder. Centre, B, which has a system typical in most areas, provided very good in-service education but this did not include courses in the effective use of the video recorder. They would have needed extra staffing to provide sufficient video resource material, but the feeling was that the inspector in charge did not consider this of sufficient importance.

RECOMMENDATIONS

The approach to the use of television which we recommend in this book does have resource implications. In the present economic climate there are many problems. It needs teachers, headteachers, inspectors and advisers to be favourable to the value of the approach if the difficulties of resource shortages are to be overcome. This needs the co-operation of the resource centre leaders, and the inspectors or Teachers' Centre Wardens responsible for in-service education, to provide the resources and the in-service training necessary to make good use of these.

COMMERCIAL PRODUCTION OF RESOURCES

At present teachers tend to rely on the television companies to provide the material that they use. Some of this is not always very suitable when the video recorder is used in the way we advocate. At present there is a very limited supply of commercial material for use in the primary school. However, if there was a demand for this, more would be provided. The problem is that schools would have difficulty in buying such material, and it would need to be provided by the resource centre and distributed to schools. Perhaps if teachers found this to be of value, schools may consider purchasing it for themselves.

In co-operation with teachers we have produced a number of video tapes. These use a modular approach which will be explained in the next chapter.

INITIAL TRAINING AND IN-SERVICE EDUCATION

Very few colleges at the moment include a course on educational television in their training of teachers. The medium is treated as something teachers will adopt and adapt to in their courses of teaching. Without guidance and awareness of the implications surrounding the use of television, it is only natural that students resort to what they feel is the way to use it when they become teachers - merely taking children to watch programmes. They would benefit from a course that emphasized how their teaching could be supplemented by the use of television, the role of the medium in the curriculum and its relationships to children's learning. A section on the effective use of the video recorder should be an essential part of such a course.

The fact that very few colleges provide training in the use of television and effective use of the video recorder must have a bearing on teachers' ineffective use of the television and video recorder, but the situation has not been corrected for the majority of teachers since they qualified. Very few in-service courses have been held at teachers' centres and colleges or have been sponsored by the DES. The use of educational television has been ignored on the assumption that television is a simple thing for teachers to use. They have been left to get on with it by themselves and only those who have evaluated the implications of the use of the medium have contemplated change. Even so, these teachers have been left to their own devices, often without the support and encouragement of people in higher positions. The existing situation reveals an urgent need for an increased in-service programme to acquaint teachers with ways in which educational television might be used more effectively with existing resources.

SUGGESTED ORGANIZATION

With the new arrangements for in-service training, LEAs will have different ideas of how this should be done. Whatever arrangements are made it would seem advisable that a member of the local resource centre and a local inspector or adviser should be involved. Teachers and headteachers in schools which are using television effectively suggest that representatives from local primary schools should form a group. This would be similar to the ways in which groups study together for the teaching of primary science, use of microcomputers, etc. The advantage would be that schools could build up resource material which they could exchange and perhaps even specialize in a certain area of work. If schools could obtain a video camera, they could film aspects of the local environment which could be useful to all the schools in the group.

THE USE OF THE VIDEO CAMERA

Although the use of the video camera was not specifically studied in the original project a small number of teachers had either used or would have liked to use it. One teacher who was particularly keen had been able to purchase a camera for use in school and it was decided to study how she had used this over the period of an academic year.

Teacher's Use of the Video Camera

The teacher was the deputy headteacher of a semi-rural endowed infant and nursery school in South Wales. She had obtained a combined camera and recorder which had cost about £1,000. Although not of professional standard it was reasonably easy to move about and not too complicated to operate. She was a competent and keen photographer but had no previous experience in operating the camera. The camera was obtained at the beginning of the autumn term and the first half-term was spent filming the children in the playground. The purpose of this was to familiarize herself with the operation of the camera and to get the children used to being filmed. After a large number of children had been allowed to make funny faces at the camera they settled down to their own activities and seemed not to be aware that they were being filmed. The tape could of course be re-used, a big advantage compared with the 16mm film camera.

In the second half of the term the school was preparing for the Christmas concert. The teacher filmed rehearsals and these were shown to the children. They were able to evaluate their own and other children's performances and even give suggestions for improvement. This made the children feel more involved and added to the general enthusiasm. A video was eventually made of the final concert.

During the rest of the year the teacher was involved in a number of projects. A local Roman museum was opened by the Duke of Gloucester and she was able to film this. She took advantage of this by getting her children to portray scenes of Roman times, e.g. Roman schools, chariot racing, children's games, etc., under the general heading of 'A Child's Life in Roman Times'. The same procedure as in the Christmas concert was adopted and the same advantages were observed. This procedure was also adopted with the St David's Day concert, and in a joint production of *Peter Rabbit* with the junior school.

The teacher also produced a tape on 'Inside and Outside our Church'. This was based on a Ladybird book, but it was far more real to the children because it was their church. She filmed an outing to the zoo. This was of particular interest because, apart from the usual shots of the children departing and arriving home, she filmed a number of animal sequences. By this time the teacher had become secretary of the group that was involved in the making of tapes by the modular approach and had spent a comparatively long time filming animals in various activities. These had been found to be a valuable teaching aid, especially as the children had seen the animals previously. She was planning to make a tape on road safety with her own class children involved, pointing out particular dangers to children in the school, and also felt confident enough to make a tape for general school use on environmental studies using a modular approach. This approach is explained in the next chapter.

All of the films had been shown at parents' evenings. They had been received enthusiastically by the parents, many of whom owned personal video recorders and who wished to purchase the tapes. If she could get them copied at a reasonable price she was prepared to do so.

FUTURE DEVELOPMENT

It must be admitted that most primary schools are not fortunate enough to own their own camera or have a teacher on the staff with as much knowledge and enthusiasm as the teacher who co-operated in this project. There are, however, a number of resource centres which are willing to provide courses or individual help in the use of the video camera, and which will lend a camera on request.

There are nevertheless problems in that although filming in schools need not be of a professional standard, many teachers would need help in using the video camera. Although this type of work is only attempted at present in a very small number of schools there is great potential in the way it can be used in primary education. It is hoped that more colleges and local authorities will provide some courses to inform teachers of the video camera's potential uses and to help teachers in filming techniques. It is likely that video cameras will become cheaper, and if a group of schools combined it may be worth buying one between them.

Chapter Seven

THE MODULAR APPROACH TO VIDEO

Questions were asked by a number of teachers about whether the material being provided by the BBC and ITV companies is suitable for the video approach using secondary stop/start procedures which we outlined in the previous chapter. Used in this way television is able to add interpretation. The children have already experienced and diagnosed but require clarification before they can deduce. Reviewing the instance on television provides the missing link for this to materialize.

BBC AND ITV PROGRAMMES

The broadcasters favour the programme approach with their material. This means that a broadcast is a complete unit within itself with a beginning middle and end. For example, a programme about a baker will show scenes of corn being harvested and ground into flour followed by the baker mixing dough, adding yeast, and dividing the dough into baking tins. The dough is shown rising in the proving oven, being baked in the baking oven, and eventually being taken out brown and steaming. The next sequence shows the loaves being sliced and wrapped, and finally being sold in the baker's shop. As such the programme has a narrative, a story to tell, and this is accompanied by voice-over explanations, or by being fronted by a presenter. Thereby, the programme is attempting to interpret what it is depicting to its audience, and, as previously instanced, it is often beyond the comprehension of many primary-school children.

A teacher using a video playback of a broadcast might attempt to deal with sequences through secondary stop/start or even basic stop/start but the format of a programme does make this awkward. She has to decide on which sequence she intends to use with the children and has to use her own judgement to find the place on the tape or by using the timing mechanism on the video. She has no time indicator on the tape itself. The voice-over description or the presenter's explanations might either interfere with or be inappropriate to the sequence. The teacher could turn down the sound but this would eliminate the natural sounds which could be essential to what is being viewed. In addition, concerned as it is with a continuum, a programme does not dwell on any particular aspect for any length of time. This means that the sequence is in insufficient depth for what the teacher requires and the pace is too quick for the children. Apart from the occasional programme made for secondary children, it does not appear that the broadcasting companies have any intention of changing their present format.

Furthermore, if a teacher is incorporating television within the curriculum, she needs material readily available when she requires it. The current week's broadcasts if videoed can be used by the secondary or basic stop/start approach but this does not imply that they will be necessarily integrated within the children's activities and work to provide follow-on. This will occur fortuitously if a broadcast happens to fit in with the activities during the week concerned or if the teacher has been selective in her choice of programme. To cater for television material to be available when it is required necessitates either establishing a resource library within the school or being at hand to borrow the relevant tape.

MODULAR APPROACH TO PROGRAMME MAKING

Each of these points arose during our research. A certain amount of dissatisfaction with the broadcast material was voiced by the teachers so it was decided to look into the matter. Seven teachers and three headteachers were assembled to form an advisory group to enquire into the provision of television material for primary school children, together with Pascal Kivotos, Head of AVE, Goldsmiths' College, University of London. Several ideas were put forward but these were closely related to programmes. The teachers were influenced by the format of educational television programmes but the intention was not to compete with the broadcasters but to produce tapes that could be used differently to enable playback and stop/start at a point which fits in with current activities. It was then agreed that the idea of programmes should be abandoned in favour of sequences of a few minutes' duration based on a theme that a teacher could use as a resource.

Water was decided upon as a theme and the main group was subdivided geographically to provide three groups to produce tapes on Movement of Water (ripples, waves, waterfalls etc.), Movement through Water (transport, fish, ducks, etc.), and Life on and Around a Pond. Each group then made its suggestions for the likely material for their topic and Pascal Kivotos agreed to undertake the filming. The filmed material was then shown to the teachers for them to decide, with guidance from the research team, what to include in the tapes. Various comments were made and suggestions agreed on the content. Movement was implicit, long-distance shots followed by close-ups were regarded as necessary, concentration on an aspect rather than a fleeting shot would allow children to look in depth. Natural sound as opposed to a musical background was preferable. Voice-over or a presenter would be a distraction rather than an asset and might also limit the age range of the children for whom it was suitable. Thus, a modular approach of various sequences, grouped under a general theme, had evolved. At the teacher's discretion, all or only part of the module could be used for viewing with a group of children while it was also possible for children to view by themselves under directions from the teacher.

Acting on the teachers' suggestions, Pascal Kivotos was responsible for editing the filmed material into the desired modules. He and the research team were able to give indications and directions on the way modules should be structured but it was the teachers who decided which material was suitable and what was required. In addition, the teachers prepared guides to accompany each tape and did not regard each module in isolation. They assessed how modular material might be linked with other topics or areas of learning with which children could be involved, and prepared an index of these. Thereby the tapes could be stored and referred to as and when they were needed.

Pilot Testing of Tapes

The teachers then tested the tapes with their children. As will be imagined, through their involvement with the Incorporating Educational Television into the Curriculum Project, small-group viewing and the secondary stop/start approach were the media of use and the following is an example of one teacher's use:

Pond-Skater, Beetle, Snail, Sequence Tape time: 4 minutes

Shown to a mixed group of children from more than one class who had been making a collection and preparing a project on sails. Ages: 5, 6 and 7 years. About eight children.

Project by two boys, Grant and Ricky, but interest has developed and spread to other children.

Video sequence shown as a result of this interest. First showing without stopping.

Immediate comment on the snail:

Grant: Why did you slow the film down?
Teacher: But I didn't.
Ricky: Do they really move out of their shells that slowly?
Teacher: Well, I'll show you again.
Repeat showing of snail sequence.
The propagator that has been a breeding home for the boys' snails is on the floor.
Ricky: Let's get our snails out and look.
Grant and Ricky take out the largest snails on to the palms of their hands and the children observe the snail trail.
Grant: Do you know where snails lay their eggs? - Well look underneath the leaf - see that jelly and see these small snails.
At this the children are invited to lift out the snails and look at them.
Ricky: Let's have a snail race.
Grant and Ricky move to a nearby table to watch the snails move - very slowly.
The other children move to the snails in the propagator and take out some of the smaller snails and turn them over.
Alan: My snail's done a poo - Look.
Other children: Look at it ... it's green.
As the snail moves over Alan's hand.
Other children: Does it tickle?
Alan: I'm going to put it back now.
Teacher: Well when you put it back you'd better wash your hands thoroughly.
Ricky: (holding his snail) Look at his tentacles - you feel them. Now they're going back - could you feel the little bump?
Snails are turned over.
Grant: Do you know how they pick up their food? Look here (pointing) they pick it up as they bend up their underneath.
At this, attention is drawn to one of the snails left on the

table and now climbing up a bookcase.

Grant: I think we'll put him back now.

Teacher: Do you remember your tadpoles? Do you want to see the film of some tadpoles?

Video sequences of tadpoles - about one and a half minutes.

Child: I've see them like that.

Teacher: Have you?

Child: There's a lot of them, isn't there?

Teacher: What do you think happens to them?

Child: Don't know.

Teacher: Well, they'll turn into frogs.

Another child: Yes, but a lot of them won't. They'll get eaten. Can we see the rest of the film?

At this they watch to the end, about nine minutes reviewing the snail sequence and seeing the dragonfly nymph, caterpillar and fisherman.

Child: Where did you make the film?

Teacher: At the pond near Staples Road - do you know it?

One child does and another thinks he does.

Interest and concentration span coming to an end.

Teacher: It's time now for you to be getting out to play.

Advantages of Modular Approach

The teachers were also asked to summarize their views on the experiment and to comment on how they saw television and the video recorder being used in the primary school classroom. One group commented that the television and video should usually be used with the stop/start playback approach, allowing for child interaction. This creates the opportunity for flexibility of viewing and for different sized groups within an integrated day method. Such groups should be organized to match (i) ability level or (ii) interest level. Methods used might be stop/start, freeze-frame, short continuous sections. There would also be opportunities for individuals or small groups to operate the video independently of the teacher. Hopefully, this would encourage:

1 Children to participate actively in the viewing.
2 Both children and the teacher to control the programme together to get maximum benefit from it.
3 Flexibility to explore situations together without being pressurized to the point where the television dictates each follow-on activity. 'Let's see that again' was a luxury

hitherto unknown.

4 The breakdown of customary once-a-week undiscerning viewing.

5 The teacher to plan ahead selectively, i.e. being aware of the content of the programme. She can select relevant parts rather than rely on one programme in its entirety.

6 Group discussion enables the teacher to discover what particularly interests individual children. This also motivates the children during the learning situation and extends vocabulary, encourages language development and observation techniques. The children themselves are setting a value on this activity and real learning is taking place.

The video/television can be viewed in a number of learning situations:

1 General interest, as an extension of the children's own experiences, e.g. a visit to a stream and an involvement with activity there.

2 As a reference for following a set of guidelines where a child might be handicapped by low reading ability, e.g. children built their own boat following a pattern used on video.

3 Open-ended problem-solving situation, e.g. children built their own weir and experimented in changing the speed of the water after seeing the Movement of Water video. Children experimented with mirrors to create reflections after viewing river sequence on the video.

4 Storytelling, a shared experience using professional storytellers; immediate visual aid to further comprehension skills.

The suggestion therefore is that use of television is considerably enhanced when the material for use is in a modular form. The continuous narrative imposed by a programme no longer exists while the material is specifically designed to concentrate on certain aspects. Using modules is more convenient than looking for appropriate breaks in programmes, saving time if replay is needed and avoiding lengthy gaps when having to play forward to find the appropriate sequence.

It is possible that teachers who have a good resource library in schools, or facilities for obtaining tapes, could use broadcast programmes in the ways shown above, but it has been found to be difficult when programmes are made in the way they are at present. However, it is essential that teachers preview programmes that they wish to use in modular form, and information which is given about the contents of each module. The main doubt expressed by the large majority of teachers was the feasibility of small-group teaching with video in a normal classroom situation. All the teachers in the small advisory group used video in this way. One of the teachers was observed doing this and a video tape was made of the lesson. Details of this lesson which would be fairly typical of the work of the teachers in the advisory group is given below.

Example of Small-group Teaching

The teacher worked in a large infant school in an inner city area of an outer London Borough. Children came from a variety of ethnic groups and the school was situated in a sociably deprived area. When the teacher was observed she was teaching in the top age group in the infant school.

School Organization for Topic Work

This school had a well-organized system for topic work. Each year group's topic work lasted for half a term, and there were quite detailed suggestions of what might be included in the topic. There were lots of resources in the school connected with the work, but this did not include video material as the school was not in possession of a video recorder. Sometimes, the topic coincided with the educational programme selected and watched by the teacher and good use was made of it. In most cases, however, the television programme was treated quite separately.

Teachers' Organization for Topic Work

Because of her involvement with the project the teacher was able to obtain a video recorder and a receiver for her use which she was able to keep in the classroom. However, when observed she had only used the video recorder for about six weeks. Her topic work was centred around water and she had organized the class into four groups of six or seven children. Each group covered four areas of the topic over a period of two or three weeks and then the areas were changed. During the observed lesson the four group activities were as follows:

1 *Art Work* Making water patterns connected with what had been on the video recording.
2 *Craft Work* Making small boats and assisting in a class project of building on a large boat.
3 *Mathematics and Scientific Work* Water activities particularly concerned with measuring, and water properties which had been suggested by previous video viewing.
4 *Writing about water patterns* Reading books connected with water and writing about it.

There were also two children using an audio recorder for language work, and two who were using the video recorder without the teachers supervision. The latter was a form of interactive video and will be discussed later.

The teacher worked through an eighty-minute period, and during this two groups worked with her using video. Each group spent approximately fifteen minutes on this activity, and the remainder of the time was spent supervising the other children.

Group Teaching with Video

Because of the modular approach and the effective use of secondary stop/start, a great deal of profitable discussion took place. The groups only consisted of six or seven children and any child who required it was able to ask for a part to be replayed. Parts of the tape were replayed and freeze-framed to assist discussion. Two or three minutes of the taped material produced about fifteen minutes' useful activity. Different groups were shown different sections of the tape according to their interests, and the discussion was matched to a child's ability. When compared with class discussion, even when the video recorder is being used by a teacher skilled in its use, there seem to be obvious advantages of the groups method. These are:

1 Children actively participating in viewing.
2 Both teacher and children control the programme to get maximum benefit from it.
3 The teacher can plan ahead selectively by being aware of the contents of the programme.
4 Group discussion enables the teacher to discover what particularly interests individual children. This also motivates the children during learning situations, extends

vocabulary, and encourages language development and observation techniques. The children themselves are setting a value on this activity and real learning is taking place.

Because the teacher had assisted in the making of the video tapes she was fully conversant with the content and did not require extra notes. When the 'Looking Around Us' video tapes are produced commercially every section of the tape will be clearly identified and information given about the content, but no instruction on how to use the tape in actual teaching will be given.

Classroom Organization

There was no problem with classroom supervision; thirty minutes was spent teaching with the video, and the rest of the time supervising groups. When the video recorder was being used all the children seemed to carry on with their own activity with the minimum amount of supervision from the teacher. She had the help of a parent in the supervision of one of the groups. It was claimed that it took two to three weeks to get children who had not experienced it previously to get used to this type of teaching. This was no different from the situation when the microcomputer was first introduced. Careful preparation was needed, but this had been necessary when she used group and individual teaching without the use of video.

Individual Interaction

One interesting development was the individual interactive use of the video. Two children came to the video when not used by the groups. Selections from a language programme were recorded. The children followed written instructions to follow-on work from the video. This was integrated into other written work they were doing. Most children in the class were able to operate the video recorder and work in this way without difficulty. The children who were observed doing this carried out the tasks without any problem. It was pointed out by the teacher that it was no more difficult than operating a microcomputer. This opens up the possibility of using the video recorder for interaction without the use of sophisticated techniques, or necessarily being used in conjunction with the microcomputer. This was the only case we observed of a teacher using it in this manner.

While we were impressed by this teacher's method, we would not like to give the impression that this is the only way modular video can be used. It is a flexible resource which can be used in a way appropriate to a teacher's particular style of teaching.

PROVISION OF MODULAR VIDEO MATERIAL

Teachers at present are restricted in the use of the modular approach, owing to a lack of suitable tapes in the modular form being available to them. The work which we described was only in pilot form and not suitable for general distribution but on the basis of the results of the experiment we have embarked on a major project to produce modular material for primary schools. Again joined by Pascal Kivotos and Dorothy Hobart (a member of our previous research team) we have been funded by DS Information Systems and the Baring Foundation to produce such video tapes. Our project, 'Video as a Curriculum Resource', aims to produce a series of video tapes with the title 'Looking Around Us'.

Although our pilot work indicated the form which the tapes should take, the question remains as to the content which is best suited for incorporation into the primary-school curriculum. We discovered that natural sequences could be used with either nursery-school children or top juniors, for this depended on the level of interpretation by the children and the teacher, but we must determine what material primary-school teachers feel will best suit their needs. This has to be resolved through collaboration with teachers.

To this end we have established working groups of primary- school teachers in six local education authorities in England and Wales. As with the pilot work, each stage of production of the video tapes will be carried out in co-operation with these teachers, along with evaluation of their use in the classroom. Amendments will be made according to children's response and teachers' reactions.

As in other work with the video recorder, in-service education will be necessary to acquaint teachers with using modular material. The project team has arranged to give a number of talks to people responsible for in-service provision in the hope that this may encourage them to provide courses for teachers.

PROVISION OF RESOURCES

In the present economic climate many schools may not feel justified in spending their limited capitation allowance in buying modular tapes which they have not used previously. In the first place the tapes could be purchased by resource centres and placed in the resource packs they send to schools for use in topic work. Because of the information provided, cataloguing should not present any problems. An instructional tape will also be provided, showing a teacher using modular material, which should help teachers but is really no substitute for in-service education. It is hoped that when schools see the value of this approach they may purchase their own tapes, which they can use when required.

While these tapes provide material for use in language work and mathematics, no investigation has been carried out about the possibilities of making modular material for specific use in these areas. The main problem would be that schools would need to purchase them as they will probably be in constant use. Used in this way there would be a need for extra video recorders and television receivers which schools may not feel that they could purchase without an increase in funding for this purpose.

Chapter Eight

FUTURE DEVELOPMENT

Examples in Chapter 2 showed how television could be used more effectively even without the use of a video recorder. Those teachers were integrating the use of television into the curriculum by carefully planning how it should be used. Unfortunately these were isolated examples and most teachers who did not have a video recorder gave little consideration to the use of television when planning the curriculum.

Nor was there a great deal of difference with schools who had possession of a video recorder. Apart from the use of the video for the purpose of timetable convenience, there were only isolated examples of schools who planned the curriculum with an idea of how television could be used more effectively. There were a few examples of teachers who used the stop/start technique to good effect. Individual teachers could improve their use of the video recorder in this way, without any increase in resources.

Choat *et al.* (1986a) explained how the video recorder could be used more flexibly in nursery and infant schools. They advocated the following: first, small-group viewing rather than class and mass viewing which appear to be the common practice; second, secondary stop/start, when a tape is previewed beforehand and stopped to allow interaction by children and interpretation by the teacher instead of a continuous playback; finally, individual interaction when children themselves use the video for tasks assigned by the teacher or to secure information which they wish to discover.

Emphasis was made that video has a greater potential than credited hitherto. Used to advantage, video could bring a new perspective into the classroom, not only in nursery and infant schools but also in junior schools. The same probably applies to secondary schools but our investigations so far have been confined only to younger children, i.e. nursery and primary schools.

A teacher has a valuable resource when video is used to its full extent. Instead of following-up with prescribed activities or work directly related to a television programme, and often extraneous to the curriculum, video enables television material to be fitted into the children's normal activities and work. This comes about when the children are engaged with whatever the teacher feels is relevant to them and the video is used to provide further explanation or interpretation with the children following on with their activities or work afterwards. In this capacity the video is a resource to assist with teaching and children's learning by providing stimulation. Television is no longer a weekly (sometimes twice- or thrice-weekly) ritual when everybody goes to watch, irrespective of individual levels of development, but a means to be fitted to children according to their needs and interests. Rather than being controlled by television the teacher is controlling television by selecting and using it when she thinks it is desirable for the children.

However, a teacher must have sufficient material at hand for video to be used in this way. At present she has to rely on the BBC and ITV companies' educational television broadcasts, for use of other material is prohibited under existing copyright laws. Added to this, someone has to video tape the broadcasts and catalogue them for easy reference when material is required. These are time-consuming and perhaps awkward operations for many teachers, and two videos are needed if any form of editing is to be undertaken.

To build up a resource library of video material is a daunting task and requires the services of a teacher who is particularly enthusiastic and interested in video techniques. We have encountered a few schools where this is happening. Alternatively, a teacher might be able to secure material from the local resource centre but there are snags to be overcome. First, the teacher will normally require the material fairly quickly. Something arises during the children's activities and she wants the video tape almost immediately, whereas material from the resource centre has to be ordered in advance. This could be avoided if the tape were permanently available in her own school. Secondly, the resource centres which we have visited carry numerous tapes suitable for secondary-school pupils but hardly any material for primary and nursery children.

These are the problems which confront teachers who wish to use television and video more effectively and they are added to by the restrictive nature of programmes. A television programme is a continuous broadcast with a beginning, middle and end, and objectives instituted by the producer. To achieve these he uses a presenter or voice-over to emphasize what is intended. Material in this form is not conducive to secondary stop/start with a video recorder when only short extracts are required.

The examples of the effective use of the video recorder illustrated in Chapter 4 show what is possible under present circumstances. However, these schools had given a great deal of thought to its use and were better equipped than the large majority of schools. Even with these advantages they had not sufficient video resources to permit teachers always to use them at the time they were required, nor were the programmes or extracts from the programmes usually conducive for secondary stop/start video recorder use, especially when only short extracts were required. The importance of in-service training must again be emphasized, especially when the number of primary schools which possess video recorders has increased to such an extent that before long nearly all primary schools will have this facility.

In an attempt to overcome some of the problems we became members of a team that embarked on a pilot study with a group of ten teachers. This has been reported in detail in Chapter 6.

The Interactive Video in Schools Project was set up to investigate the potential of the video disc player (Plummer 1987a, 1987b). It was considered that the convergence of two technologies, video and computing, created a learning and teaching aid which was flexible to the needs of both student and teacher. Eight packages are being designed and produced by practising teachers and, the video material having been completed, the software is being completed and piloted in over a hundred schools. Much of the software has been designed to enable teachers to tailor the material within a package to their own requirements without losing the overall structure of a 'program'. Each package has been designed to run in conjunction with existing micros in schools and to accommodate several different disc players. Plummer points out that pupils are using the software provided to produce their own interpretation of the visual materials and stresses that the obvious conclusion is that the potential of the material is virtually unlimited and that development of software beyond a certain stage must lie with schools themselves.

It seems from Plummer's summaries that a structure exists within the packages. No mention is made of how the video material was chosen but it would appear that this was formulated to achieve certain objectives and to conform to a programme principle. For instance, of the eight packages only one is designed specifically for use with primary-school children. The package deals with an aspect of primary science which Plummer claims is 'difficult to attack in the classroom not only because of the physical constraints but also because it deals with a level of knowledge beyond that of most primary school teachers, yet it is fundamental to all physical science'. Solar energy and its effect on all aspects of life therefore is the topic and the package continually guides children from the visual material into practical activities which are supported by worksheets into manifestations of energy such as photosynthesis, colour panels, food chains and webs, respiration, consumption, etc. The package encompasses work over three terms and is designed to integrate with the investigative, research orientated approach to science in the primary school.

Although the intention is to incorporate the material into the curriculum and to encourage practical work, the impression is gained that, through the underlying structure of the programme, the package attempts to regulate what should be happening in primary school classrooms. In some respects this is not detrimental for it supports those teachers with a fragmentary knowledge of science, but there are certain drawbacks.

Plummer gives no indication of the form of the visual material, whether it is modular or otherwise. It is most likely tailored to meet learning objectives instituted in the package. Latitude is allowed for teachers to develop their own software but the computer 'program' is geared towards attaining the learning objectives. Emphasis therefore would appear to be on the computer side with video playing a subsidiary role. Piloting in over a hundred schools suggests that each of these schools is fully equipped, including a disc player, to carry out the function, but the question remains as to whether primary schools in general will be prepared to meet the cost of purchasing a disc player. In addition they must be assured that an adequate amount of material will be available to use with the player, but even this will cost money. The one package from the Interactive Video in School Project must be supplemented from many sources to justify the outlay.

The video disc player therefore is unlikely to have an immediate impact in primary schools. On the other hand, with three-quarters of primary schools possessing a video recorder, there is every justification for providing material not only to encourage more flexible use of the medium but also to fill the void which exists. In other words, suitably prepared software for the video recorder would encourage interactive video prior to the use of the more sophisticated video player. Furthermore, it can be said that video-recorder modular tape material has different objectives than those which have emanated from the video disc.

First, it is a resource which can be fitted into children's activities and work according to needs and interests. Second, there is no structured programme to abide by. The material is open-ended with no specific learning objective. Third, it is fulfilling a need by providing readily accessible material when required by either teacher or children. Fourth, emphasis is on the video pictures and there is no undue concern created by the computing side. Although video-recorder recall is not as swift as the disc player, its digital numbers enable modules to be fairly quickly located. Finally, and most importantly, interaction between television teacher and children becomes a reality. As Choat *et al.* (1987) indicate, little is known of what young children do learn from television when they sit before a screen without any form of interaction. Because of its format a modular tape encourages small-group viewing. A teacher is then able to assess each child's reaction, clarify doubts and misunderstandings brought about by television techniques or distortions, intervene to challenge children, and stimulate learning according to needs and interests.

In conclusion we are of the opinion that schools would find the use of modular tapes provided by DS Information Systems and outlined in the previous chapter very valuable, but much work needs to be done to enable teachers to use the present television programmes provided in the best way. As teachers become more proficient in the use of the video they will see the need for more sophisticated approaches, which may encourage schools and local authorities to provide extra resources and also the in-service education that is required. We welcome the support provided for research into interactive video. While in the short term it does not seem a practicable proposition because of the high cost of the video disc player and the lack of sufficient software, it could be a very effective way of teaching if these problems could be overcome.

REFERENCES

Cabinet Office Information Technology Advisory Panel (1986) *Learning To Live with IT*, London: HMSO.
Choat, E., Griffin, H. and Hobart, D. (1986a) 'Video recorder

use in nursery and infants' schools', *Head Teachers' Review*, Autumn: 31-2.

Choat, E., Griffin, H. and Hobart, D. (1986b) 'Educational television and the curriculum for children up to the age of seven years', *British Journal of Educational Technology*, 3: 164-73.

Choat, E., Griffin, H., and Hobart, D. (1987) *Teachers and Television* Beckenham: Croom Helm.

Plummer, B. (1987a) 'The IVIS League', *The Times Educational Supplement* 23 January, p. 35.

Plummer, B. (1987b) 'Interactive video in schools', *CET News*, May, pp. 10-11.

INDEX